Stories from My Life

Novels

Sounding Brass	Late Have I Loved Thee
Green Willow	Every Man a Stranger
Crescendo	Bavarian Story
Children of the Earth	At Sundown, the Tiger
Ragged Banners	The Fields at Evening
Linda Shawn	Love Under Another Name
Venetian Blinds	The Living Lotus
Men Are Unwise	Pity the Innocent
Cactus	Fragrance of Hyacinths
The Pure Flame (*Sequel to* Cactus)	The Blue-eyed Boy
Women Also Dream	Sabishisa
Rose and Sylvie	Curfew at Dawn
Darkness My Bride	The Road to Beersheba
Julie	The Burning Bush
Rolling in the Dew	The Night and its Homing
Red Rose (*Emma Goldman*)	The Lady and the Mystic
Captain Moonlight	Bitter Babylon
The Blossoming Bough	The Midnight Street
Proud Heaven	Free Pass to Nowhere
Lucifer and the Child	The Curious Adventure of Major Fosdick
The Dark Forest	Mission to Beirut
Comrade O Comrade!	*Etc.*

Politics and Ethics

Women and the Revolution (*Secker & Warburg*)	Rebels' Ride (*the revolt of the individual*)
Bread and Roses (*Macdonald*)	Loneliness (*a study of the human condition*)
Commonsense and Morality	Practitioners of Love (*some aspects of the human phenomenon*)
Christianity—or Chaos?	

Short Stories

Green Figs	No More Mimosa
Dryad	The Wild Swans (*three tales based on the Ancient Irish*)
The Falconer's Voice	
So Tiberius . . . (*a novella*)	

Travels and Memoirs

Confessions and Impressions	Brief Voices (*a writer's story*)
South to Samarkand	The Flowery Sword (*travels in Japan*)
Privileged Spectator (*sequel to Confessions and Impressions*)	A Lance for the Arabs (*a Middle East journey*)
Moroccan Mosaic	Aspects of Egypt
Two Studies in Integrity (*Gerald Griffin and 'Father Prout'*)	The Lovely Land (*The Hashemite Kingdom of Jordan*)
Land of the Crested Lion (*a journey through modern Burma*)	An American Journey
Connemara Journal	England for a Change
German Journey	England at Large
Jungle Journey (*India*)	Young in the Twenties (*a chapter of autobiography*)
This Was a Man (*some memories of Robert Mannin*)	England My Adventure
The Country of the Sea (*some wanderings in Brittany*)	*Etc.*

Child Education

Commonsense and the Child	Ann and Peter in Austria (*Muller*)
Commonsense and the Adolescent	Ann and Peter in Japan (*Muller*)
Ann and Peter in Sweden (*Muller*)	With Will Adams through Japan (*Muller*)

Cat Books

The Saga of Sammy-Cat (*Pergamon Press*)	My Cat Sammy (*Michael Joseph*)

The author in her garden

ETHEL MANNIN

Stories from My Life

HUTCHINSON OF LONDON

HUTCHINSON & CO (*Publishers*) LTD
3 Fitzroy Square, London W1

London Melbourne Sydney Auckland
Wellington Johannesburg Cape Town
and agencies throughout the world

First published 1973

*This book has been set in Baskerville type, printed in Great Britain
on antique wove paper by Anchor Press, and
bound by Wm. Brendon, both of Tiptree, Essex*

ISBN 0 09 116590 3

For
JOE O'HALLORAN
in abiding friendship

Contents

PART I: IRELAND

1 Farewell to Connemara   13
2 Her Excellency Regrets   23
3 Burmese Buddha via Ireland   31
4 Japanese Garden, Kildare   35

PART II: THE MIDDLE EAST

1 Down on the Gulf: Kuwait   45
2 Making a Film with the Arabs   62
3 A *mansaf* with the Beersheba *bedu*   77
4 Incident by the Barada river, Damascus   86
5 The Children's Things   90

PART III: GREEK STEAMER TO ALEX, 1964

1 Venice Revisited   99
2 Greek Steamer   106
3 Athens and the Acropolis   110
4 A Glimpse of Rhodes   116

8 *Contents*

PART IV: PARIS INTERLUDE, 1971

PART V: ENGLAND

1	My Burglar, Mr. Stanley	137
2	Young Man in a Parma Violet Shirt	146
3	Race Relations	152
4	Long Day's Journey into Windsor	156
5	At the Concert	160
6	The Little Feller	163
7	Uninvited Guest	169

PART VI: PORTRAIT OF A YOUNG REVOLUTIONARY
In Memoriam

1	Dissident Iraqis	179
2	Khalid	186
3	The Marshes	191

PART VII: THE CONTINUING STORY

1	Three-Score-Years-and-Ten	197
2	The Quiet Rhythm	203
3	At Close of Play	211

EPILOGUE: 1973

Index	221

Illustrations

The author in her garden *(Paul Tanqueray)*   *frontispiece*

Island View Cottage, Connemara   *facing page* 32

Shri and Shrimati Bhalla with Shivaramakrishnan
  at the Galway Literary Society, 1960 *(Connacht
  Tribune)*   32

The Burmese Buddha that came via Ireland *(F. W.
  Ziemsen)*   33

Kuwait: general view   48

Kuwait: the Secondary School   48

Author speaking at Qalqiya, Jordan, April 1965   49

The black tents of the *bedu (Radio Times Hulton
  Picture Library)*   49

Guard at the Royal Palace, Athens *(The National
  Tourist Organisation of Greece)*   112

House of Commons, 1969. Dame Peggy Ashcroft;
  Anne Kerr, M.P.; the author; Betty Ambatielos   113

Rhodes: The Castle of the Knights *(The National
  Tourist Organisation of Greece)*   113

The Byron Monument at the National Park, Athens
  (Alfa Tourist and Travel Agency, Athens)   128

'To Paris in June, 1971, to meet my old friend
  Rickey Austin . . .'   129

'The old house in the rue Cassini . . .' *facing page* 129

Author with her burglar, Frank Stanley, at Norman
House, 1962   144

Reginald Reynolds wearing his 'burglar suit'   144

Sammy, the 'little feller' *(F. W. Ziemsen)*   145

Oak Cottage, to which the author came in 1929
(Humphrey and Vera Joel)   145

General Abdel Karim Qassim, Prime Minister of
Iraq   160

Khalid Zaki, Iraqi revolutionary, killed in May 1968   160

Sheikh Abdulla Al-Salim Al-Sabah, Emir of Kuwait,
1962   160

'Tim' (F. W. Ziemsen) at Oak Cottage *(Paul
Tanqueray)*   161

Oak Cottage *(F. W. Ziemsen)*   161

PART I
Ireland

I

Farewell to Connemara

In recent years so many people have asked me if I still have my Irish cottage, and have seemed disappointed, and also puzzled, when I have said that no, I sold it lock, stock and barrel, for a song, in 1962 and have never regretted it, that this seems the place to tell the story of the reason-why. Then if anyone else asks me I can refer them to chapter one of this book, and I need never think of it or speak of it again—which I would prefer.

There are stories in the lives of all of us which are pleasant to recall—with nostalgia, or a gentle amusement; we remember and are glad. Conversely there are the experiences we would much prefer to forget, and from which, remembering, we turn sideways with distaste. Such is the story of my farewell to Connemara after seventeen years during which I knew much happiness and peace there, and which were in the nature of a love-affair. But love-affairs with places can come to an end, bitter at that, no less than with people, and the more intense the love the greater can be the bitterness at the end.

How deeply I loved the peace and beauty of Connemara is most lyrically set forth in my *Connemara Journal*, published in 1947, and in my Irish Catholic novel, *Late Have I Loved Thee,* published two years later, both of them written there. At that time, under the insidious influence of Irish Catholicism—of living, that is to say, a good deal of the time in so strongly Catholic an environment—I had one foot over the threshold of the Church of Rome, but as my Quaker husband, the late Reginald Reynolds, put it, with intense relief, 'fortunately the traffic lights turned to red this side of Vatican City.' I did a great deal of Catholic reading at that time, and had a number of conversations with Irish Catholic priests of different orders—Redemptorists, Jesuits, Franciscans—but when it came to it I was not capable of the willing suspension of disbelief; of 'the faith that precedes reason'. Or, as the Irish say, more simply, I was not given the Grace. Despite all their prayers.

How I found and rented the cottage, a few miles from Mannin Bay, I have told in *Connemara Journal*. That was in 1938. I was not allowed to go there during the war years, despite repeated applications to the Home Office, and did not get back until 1945. From then on I went over two or three times a year for some seventeen years, although already by 1949 I was beginning to weary of the sheer effort of these journeyings—by train to Liverpool; the night-crossing from Liverpool, which got me to Dublin in good time for the eight o'clock train from Westland Row station to Galway, where I would arrive at midday; I would lunch and shop in Galway and get the five o'clock 'bus to Clifden—there being none earlier—which took two-and-a-half or three hours to cover the fifty miles, according to whether the route was via Roundstone or not; the thing was not to arrive in Galway on the day when it was 'the Roundstone route'—though, mind you, that offered the finest scenery. But there comes a point when scenery is not everything. Arrived at Clifden it was still not the end of the journey, for the cottage was two miles outside of that two-street capital of Connemara, so the last lap was done by local taxi, and by the time you arrived, sometime after eight in the evening, after leaving London the previous afternoon, you had had enough. Indeed you had. People would ask, 'Why don't you fly to Dublin?' The answer to which was that it wouldn't help, since the necessity was to catch the 8 a.m. train out to Galway, in order to arrive in Clifden and reach the cottage by the evening. Flying to Dublin would have meant spending a night there, adding to the expense, which was considerable without that.

There was that, then, the sheer exhaustion of the journey, plus the expense, plus the increasing tedium of it, plus the fact that every time I returned all the labour I had put into the half acre of wild land I had made into some sort of a garden would be lost; I would leave it reasonably neat and tidy and return to find it a weedgrown wilderness, whilst in the house the damp, with which I waged such endless—and such expensive—battles would have taken over again. The return would always be at the outset a very disheartening affair; there was always the feeling of having to start more or less from scratch again. By the time I left, of course, after about a month, I would have got everything, indoors and out, to rights, and everything would be looking very nice. But I would get back to London to find the garden at Oak Cottage had gone to pot in my absence. The truth being, of course, that you cannot live in two places, and many times between 1949 and 1962 I had thought of selling the place—which I had bought when I returned in 1945—but always when I returned the peace and beauty of the place wooed me anew.

But not in 1962.

By the summer of 1962 I had not been back for twelve months. In June, 1961, I became a grandmother, and in the face of that exciting and important event had no inclination at all to do other than stay put. Early next year would be soon enough to return to Connemara; the spring, even; there really was no hurry. A developing political interest in Middle East affairs was also to some extent undermining my enthusiasm for isolating myself in the wilds of Connemara. Early in 1962 I received an invitation from General Qassim's government to be their guest in Iraq; I accepted this invitation, and flew to Baghdad; this led to invitations from other Arab governments to be an official guest in their countries, and I became involved in an extensive tour of the Middle East, and when I returned to London, some two months later, was busy with the book about it, *A Lance for the Arabs*,* and not until this was off my hands—by which time my grand-daughter was a year old—did I feel free, or even want, to return to Connemara.

It was always my custom when returning to let my neighbours, who lived some distance along the lane, know some days in advance, so that they could go in and open the place

* 1963.

up, airing it, and restoring some order to the area around the house. Always, too, on the evening I got back one of them would come down to greet me, usually Herself, to inquire was everything all right, and how was I, at all.

But not this time.

The usual things had been done—the grass scythed, a fire lit, a jug of milk left; but no one called down, so that it was a lonely and unwelcoming return after twelve months. I was surprised, and I was hurt. I had kept in touch with them during my long absence, writing frequently, and had assumed they would be even more delighted to see me back after a year away than after the usual few months. Why not? I had been a good friend to them down through the years, and always when I returned paid without question whatever they stated was owing for services rendered in my absence.

But no one looked in that evening, nor the following day, and at the end of that long, lonely day, during which I saw no one and spoke to no one, I decided to paint the iron gate at the bottom of the drive up to the house, it having become very rusty in my absence. I always liked painting the gate, because at the other side of the lane there were bouldery fields going down to the estuary, flanked at the far side by the gorse-covered ridge of Errislannan, and there would be the cry of curlews underlining the silence; but that evening I wanted to paint the gate in the hope of someone passing up or down the lane and exchanging a few friendly words—if it was only to observe that it was a fine evening.

When I had been brushing on the paint for a little while my neighbour came along on her bicycle. I straightened up to greet her, as she approached, welcoming the prospect of a chat.

'Hullo, then,' she called, as she came close—and to my astonishment did not descend from her bicycle but rode on down the lane.

I guessed that she was on her way to the nearby guest-house; she went for an hour or two in the evenings during the tourist season to help with the washing-up. I told myself that perhaps she was a little late and did not want to be further delayed by stopping to gossip with me; she would no doubt stop for a chat on her way home.

I went on painting and no one else passed; an hour or so
later I was still at it when she rode back, and again I straightened up.

'Still working!' she called—and cycled on.

I finished the gate, wiped my brush, picked up the can of
paint and walked up the drive and into the house, completely
bewildered; stunned.

So that it was it, then; they simply were not interested in my
return. I had stayed away too long.

In the morning I walked up the lane to their cottage, paid them
what they asked for that they had done about the place,
admired their neatly trimmed box hedges, gossiped a little.
They were friendly enough, asked me in; outwardly all was the
same, but the old affectionate warmth had gone. I had never
really belonged, I suppose; only had the wishful-thinking
illusion of it. I was English and an outsider, fundamentally.
And I had not been there for a year. Oh, well.

The week passed; I worked in the garden, cutting back over-
grown bushes, grubbing out weeds and brambles; there was
always a great deal to do on that half acre of rough bouldery
land in which I had carved out a few flower beds and borders.
Beyond the monkey-puzzle tree I had planted back in the
forties a track led down through a confusion of fuchsia and
blackberry bushes to the pine wood that was part of the estate,
and keeping this track clearly defined was a 'thing' with me,
so that I was always cutting back brambles and hawthorns to
that end, and it afforded me a curious satisfaction. I liked to
walk down that narrow path to the wood, and keeping it clear
somehow made the wild land less of a wilderness—gave it,
even, some pretensions to being a garden; landscaped, at that.
I was always cutting down brambles in the wood, too, and
I liked being in there among the tall trees, gathering wheel-
barrow loads of sticks for starting the turf fire every morning—
and wheeling the loads of kindling up to the turf shed was
another reason for keeping the path to the wood clear.

Well, there was plenty to do; every morning the turf barrel
had to be filled and lugged into the house, and water fetched
from the spring in the field across the road—the rain-water

B

barrel at the back door served for general domestic purposes, but for making tea and cooking the spring water was preferable. Then there were the oil lamps to fill and the wicks to trim, and the fireplace ashes to rake out and the fire to re-lay. The 'simple life' involves a great many chores, which, once the novelty and satisfaction of being able to 'cope' wears off, become tedious. One 'mod con' I had achieved in the last couple of years—a calor-gas cooker, and in the bathroom I had had made out of what was once the shed for a donkey I had installed a ten gallon water cylinder with calor-gas jets connected with it; to heat water for the bath involved filling the cylinder from the water barrel, which entailed, of course, a good deal of to-ing and fro-ing with jugs, and standing on a chair to pour the water in; the water then took about an hour to heat, but one lay in the hot bath eventually with a tremendous sense of achievement. But it was not something to do more than once a week; not only was the sheer physical effort too great, but the rain-water barrel would not have pro-provided sufficient water for a daily bath except in a very rainy season.

The days were busy enough with all these chores, indoors and out, and at night I sat typing by the light of an Aladdin lamp. I saw no one but the postman at mid-day; he collected as well as delivered and his call would be the one event of the day. He was friendly and cheerful and welcomed me back; he was my social life and my contact with the outside world.

At the end of the week I walked the two miles into the town for some shopping and gossiped a bit in the shops; they were friendly and welcoming—I was after all a good customer when 'in residence', like all who came in from 'outside'. They'd heard I'd 'gone foreign' in the long time I'd been away and inquired about my travels; but it's not easy to talk about Baghdad, Damascus, Beirut, Amman, Cairo, Kuwait to people who have never even been to England. I had been travelling in the Arab countries, I said. Ah, the Arab countries, they said vaguely, and you could almost see behind their eyes visions of camels and palm trees and deserts and people wrapped in sheets. Aren't you great, now? they said, admiringly. I showed them snapshots of my grand-daughter and they exclaimed suitably, and even declared they could see a likeness to myself. . . .

I didn't go in again on Sunday for Mass; I was long through with all that, so the Saturday chat in the shops was all the chat there was, and all the social intercourse, for on Sunday there was not even the postman.

But what there was, as it turned out, was a storm. One of those fearful storms that sweep in from the Atlantic and ravage the landscape with howling winds for days on end. And the Atlantic was just at the bottom of the lane.

There was no one and nothing else, but there was the storm, and it brought down several of the tall pine trees in the wood. They crashed down and lay across the stone walls that bounded the wood by the roadside, partly smashing them, for they were of 'dry stone', that is to say built of stones piled one upon another but not cemented. These dry-stone walls are common throughout the West of Ireland; they are very skilfully built, but the stones are very readily dislodged, and I was continually having the wall along the road rebuilt; now a large part of it was smashed, and, with the great trees lying across the heaps of stones, presented a most desolate scene, and I was very anxious to get the trees removed and the wall rebuilt. I made local inquiries and was told the name of a contractor who would, I was assured, undertake at least the removal of the fallen trees, and getting the wall rebuilt presented no problem—it would be easy enough to find someone to do that.

I telephoned the contractor, and sure he would come; tomorrow, or the next day. But the days went by and he did not come. I telephoned again, and he said that he would come, tomorrow, or the day after. But he did not come the next day, or the day after that, or the following day, and by the end of the week I had suddenly had enough. I had been there for two weeks, and I was lonely, and bored, and frustrated, and, simply, *fed up*. The distant view of the Roundstone Mountain across the estuary, which I saw from my front door, was as beautiful as ever in its misty blue, and the evening cry of the curlews was as moving; there was the wonderful living silence, and the splendour of the crimson tide of fuchsia along the hedgerows, but for the first time in my long association with Connemara I was homesick. Scenery was no longer enough; I wanted *people*; people I could talk to and who would know what I was talking about; people who if they had less charm had also a great deal more reliability, so that if they said they would come and do a job on a certain day would come and do it. I used to return to Ireland, the land of my ancestors, with a sense of homecoming; but not any more. The long love-affair with Ireland was ended.

Even so, I did not know when I fled from Connemara at the end of a fortnight in that summer of 1962 that I would never return. I left everything, as always. I handed in the keys to my neighbours, as always, the keys of the front door and the back door, of the padlocks of the turf shed and the chain I always put on the front gate when leaving. I had to go back to England, I said. I didn't know when I'd be back. I'd be writing. If anyone came about the trees perhaps they'd let me know. They expressed surprise at my sudden departure. 'Ye didn't stay long this time,' they said, but it was a reproach rather than a regret.

The day after I left the contractor moved in, and he did not remove the trees brought down by the storm but standing timber. This I knew from a telegram sent by the Englishman who ran the nearby guest-house, and whose own bit of woodland faced across to mine. 'Contractor moving living trees from wood contact gardai immediately to stop work,' he wired me.

I immediately wired the gardai, the local police. There followed a series of telegrams. The raping of the wood was stopped. The contractor withdrew, leaving the fallen trees still lying across the tumbled walls. My English neighbour wrote, full of indignation about what he called 'the rape of the wood'; the contractor wrote full of explanations that did not explain; the gardai wrote, awaiting further instructions. But I no longer felt anger or dismay; only a bottomless disgust. I did not have to make any decisions; I knew that I would not go back. That it was all over.

I wrote my English neighbour that I was quitting; that I proposed to sell the place 'fully furnished', and if he knew of anyone likely to be interested he could put that person in touch

—only, I said, I would prefer to sell to an Irish person, and to someone who would really live there, not just use the place as a holiday home, or to let to summer visitors; it was after all something I had created, and during seventeen years I had put a great deal of work, not to say money, into both house and garden.

The Englishman was sympathetic; he was sorry I was going but understood how I felt; the rape of the wood was shocking; but if I was serious about selling he knew someone who had a friend in Dublin, who had seen the place on her visits to Connemara and been enchanted by it; she would almost certainly jump at the chance to buy it. . . .

The wheels were set in motion and I sold it to her for thirteen hundred pounds—a thousand for the freehold of the house and land, three hundred for the contents, only having a friend go in and crate my books and a few knick-knacks for shipment to England. The Dublin woman was overjoyed; she wrote me that she would try to keep up the garden as I had, and she and her husband would live there all the time, it would be their *home*—I need have no fears on that score. She was thinking of changing the name from Island View Cottage to Mannin Cottage. . . .

Fine, fine. Except, I said, not to change the name. There was Island View House, to which the Redemptorist student priests came every summer, and this was the cottage of the Big House, Island View Cottage. It was as unlucky to change the name of a house as the name of a boat. Apropos of which, I said, I was giving my sailing-dinghy, *Kathleen,* to my neighbour, so that he could go fishing for mackerel in the estuary . . . but as it turned out *Kathleen* rotted away on the beach, like so many other boats on Connemara beaches, and when I heard that this was happening I wrote asking if the brass nameplate could be sent to me, as a memento of the good days when the little boat sat so prettily on the water, gently rocking, like a red and blue bird. It was duly sent to me, and sometimes I look at it and remember, and am sad.

Duly, too, the crates of my books completed their long journey to London, to Oak Cottage, arriving pungent with the Connemara mildew on their casings, and glad, I think, to be home and dry, poor things. It is quite terrible what Connemara does to books.

That is not quite the end of the story.

Within a year an advertisement appeared in the properties-for-sale columns of a Galway newspaper : *Connemara cottage for sale, fully furnished; previously the residence of a well-known writer. Price two thousand pounds.* The friend who spotted it wrote in reply to the advertisement. It was Island View Cottage all right.

I learned later that it was not sold. What has happened to it since I do not know, and prefer not to know. But an Irish friend who saw it after I left reported that a great many of the screening shrubs had been cut down, and it was now 'just a Connemara cottage like any other'.

End of story.

2

Her Excellency Regrets

Galway, the capital of the county, and the 'gateway to the West,' is a town I always liked, small and busy, with its narrow main street winding down to the Spanish Arch, beside the harbour, where the Corrib bubbles and froths out into Galway Bay. I always enjoyed the few hours I spent there when arriving by train from Dublin on my way out to Clifden; the smell of turf fires on the mild air the moment one emerged from the station was always exciting and somehow heart-stirring. On the return journey I would get the five o'clock 'bus in from Clifden and spend the night in Galway, in the huge station hotel, the Great Southern, continuing on to Dublin in the morning, and I would always ask for a room at the top of the building, so that I had a good view out over Galway Bay to the misty blue hills of Clare.

Occasionally, when 'in residence' at the cottage, I would come in from Clifden on the early morning 'bus for a day's shopping in Galway, and entering the town over the old grey bridge across the river, the Salmon Weir Bridge, with the Gothic pile of the University on the left, and the high gaunt walls of the long disused prison on the right, was always happiness. Today, Galway Cathedral stands on the site of the old prison, and the high walls are no more, so the approach to Galway City is still finer. I have not seen the Cathedral, for it was not dedicated until 1965, but I have seen the salmon massed below the 'salmon bridge' in season, on their way upstream, packed so close that, as they say locally, you couldn't throw a stone without hitting one; and I knew the Claddagh, where the fishermen lived, when it was a huddle of bee-hived-shaped thatched cottages—as picturesque as they were insanitary. The old Claddagh disappeared—except on the picture postcards—even in my time, to be replaced by neat little square boxes of houses with the basic mod cons of electric light and running water, but the older generation turned a cold eye on this manifestation of 'progress', for sure, wasn't it all right the way it was, with the turf fires and the oil lamps and the earth closet, without all those new-fangled switches and taps and things, with nothing to go wrong, no pipes to freeze, no wires to fuse, but everything plain and simple and *natural.* . . .

The Spanish Arch, too, has been tidied up since my time, and is no longer a dilapidated ruin but part of Galway City Museum, which I am sure is right and proper, like doing away with the slummy old Claddagh, but I am of those who like the angels—even the scruffy ones—to keep their ancient places.

There was a flourishing Literary Society in Galway from 1944, and I twice had the honour of addressing it; on the first occasion I gave a light-hearted talk on How I Became a Writer, which I delivered extempore, and which, I am told, is remembered to this day as one of the highlights of the Society's twenty odd years of existence; on the second occasion I read a paper on W. B. Yeats, some personal reminiscences, but, sure, wasn't it more amusing when I just talked about meself, and them roarin' with laughter . . . or so they said, God love them, and they were probably right.

The Society's lectures were always given in a room in the hotel; they were well-attended, and each occasion was something of a social as well as a cultural event. Galway had an intelligentsia in those days. Yet Clare Sheridan, the sculptress and author, who bought a tall, shabby old house known as 'Kelly's lodging house', down by the Spanish Arch, and converted it, at vast expense, into an elegant and sophisticated home, the like of which has never been seen before in Galway City, and was a great wonder, with pillars each side of the front door, with kind of stone pineapple things atop, the way ye'd never recognise Kelly's old house at all . . . Clare Sheridan,

I was saying, received into the Catholic Church and a lay Franciscan, quit Galway after a few years and went back to her house somewhere in the Sahara, and it silted up with sand, because, she declared, the weather was awful, and there was no conversation. I would agree there was a powerful amount of rain, mind you; it seemed always to be raining in Galway City, whatever it was doing anywhere else in the West, but that there was any shortage of conversation I would deny. Faith, they'd talk ye black in the face on anything you were minded to discuss, for with its University, its Gaelic Theatre, its Literary Society, Galway was nothing if not a cultural city, in those days, intellectually lively. I, anyhow, always found it so, and I never minded the soft Irish rain. But since 1966 the Literary Society is no more, alas, and I am told that good conversation is now in short supply West of the Shannon. Present-day Ireland is cleaner, tidier, more efficient, as it moves steadily into the mainstream of 'progress', but vastly less amusing. It is, in fact becoming deadly dull, they tell me. O Synge! O Yeats! O Oliver St. John Gogarty!

I came to know the young secretary of the Galway Literary Society, Patrick Joseph O'Halloran, commonly known as Joe, who had taken over in 1949; some years later I attended his wedding in Cork, but that is another story; the story with which I am here concerned is the non-event of the cancelled visit to Galway of Mrs. Pandit, High Commissioner for India at that time, 1960, to address the Galway Literary Society, and in which I was involved, since it was through me that the invitation to her was made.

I had met Lakshmi Vijaya Pandit, the sister of Jawaharlal Nehru, when she first came to London as High Commissioner in January, 1955. I met her at the reception and dinner given for her by the Indian Social Club; there was mutual liking, and the added bond of the fact that her brother was an old friend of Reginald's, and soon after our first meeting she came to tea at Oak Cottage and a friendship was established. At the time when she was invited to address the Galway Literary Society she had attended various functions in Dublin in her role as Ambassador to Ireland, so why, Galway demanded, in the person of the secretary of the Literary Society, wouldn't she similarly honour the West? And since she was a personal friend of mine why wouldn't I put it to her that if she would come to Galway City and talk to the Literary Society about India, from any angle she chose, the intelligentsia of that city, by no means less intellectual than that of Dublin, would be honoured, delighted, and grateful. . . .

I put it to her in those terms, suggesting, also, that it would be both interesting and pleasant for her to see something of the West of Ireland, as part of her 'parish', as she called it, and it was good to be able to report back to Joe O'Halloran that Her Excellency had written me that she would be very happy to visit Galway City and address its Literary Society. Whereupon there was great rejoicing amongst the Society's members, and Joe took off to Dublin to discuss the arrangements with the Chargé D'Affaires at the Indian Embassy, and His Excellency's secretary, Rattan Bhalla, in turn took off for Galway for a personal inspection of the conditions to which Madame would be submitted, and these being found satisfactory a date in October was agreed upon for the great visit.

Galway City, with a proper impatience of Dublin, which hogged all the visiting celebrities and the limelight, and had hitherto had the Indian Ambassador to Ireland all to itself, left no stone unturned, no avenue unexplored, in its plans to honour the distinguished visitor. At the railway station, suitably decorated with the flags and national colours of the Republic of India and the Republic of Ireland, Her Excellency would be received by all the leading local lights, and outside the station a military reception would await her, and she would be royally escorted the few steps to the hotel, where the red carpet—yards and yards of it, and it of the very best quality procurable—would have been unrolled all the way to the V.I.P. suite, the largest, loftiest, most handsome rooms in the hotel, filled for the occasion with the most beautiful, the most expensive, and most exquisitely arranged flowers.

The hotel was, of course, fully apprised of the fact that Her Excellency, as a Hindu of the High Brahmin caste, was a strict vegetarian, so that she would be in no wise affronted by the food offered, which would be not only vegetarian but of a very high order.

It was not necessary to apprise the distinguished local lady, Mrs. Tona Prendergast, who was to give a reception at her house, just outside Galway City, for Madame, as they called her, for she was an India Old Hand; her late husband, Professor Prendergast, has built railways in India, and they had lived in Delhi for many years. House guests at Mrs. Prendergast's at that time were two other India Old Hands, Colonel—late of the Royal Engineers of the Indian Army—and Mrs. Cotton; and with all these Indian associations the idea of Mrs. Prendergast giving a reception for the Indian Ambassador to Ireland on her visit to Galway City seemed not only right and proper but a very nice idea. The Prendergast house, by the sea, at Salthill, at the end of the promenade, was a fine place, called Solerno, and for the occasion the façade of the house, and also the garden surrounding the house, was to be floodlit. The guests at the reception would be the cream of Galway society; the refreshment offered both suitable and exquisite; and that there would be red carpet and striped awning to the front door went without saying.

Altogether, and in all respects, all that a city could do to honour a distinguished guest Galway City arranged to do, on both the civic and social level.

Then on the morning of the day before Her Excellency was expected to arrive I received a telegram that she was unwell and unable to travel and was sending the press attaché from London, Shivaramakrishnan, also someone from the embassy in Dublin.

When I had sufficiently recovered from the shock I telephoned the O'Halloran house in Galway. Joe was not there, but I spoke to his wife.

'Bad news, Mary,' I said. 'I've just had a wire from Mrs. Pandit. She isn't coming. She's sending someone from London. Joe must know at once.'

There was a cry at the other end of the line.

'My God! The news will kill him!'

'It won't,' I assured her. 'People don't die so easily. But he must know immediately. Can you get hold of him? Tell him to ring me.'

I was on the telephone at the cottage, and provided there

had been no storm and the line hadn't blown down, it worked. Fortunately it was working then, and in due course Joe rang.

He was distressed, but remarkably calm.

'This is terrible news, all right,' he said, quietly. 'And coming at the last minute like this. But we have to go through with it—put a good face on it.'

'I happen to know the young man she is sending,' I told him. 'Jean and I knew him in India in 1949, and I met him again in London. He is very nice. People will like him.'

'I know,' he said, in the Irish way. 'But the whole of Galway is expecting a beautiful Indian lady in a glamorous sari, not an Indian young man in a lounge suit. He is also not the High Commissioner for India, nor the Ambassador to Ireland.'

'Once they're over the shock they'll like him,' I insisted. 'He's very good looking. He also has a great deal of charm.'

Over the line the fifty miles from Galway to Clifden I heard the heavy sigh.

'We can only do our best. I'll try to get word around. You'll be in Galway tomorrow evening to meet the train as arranged?'

'Of course. I'll send Mrs. Pandit a telegram of regret and condolence.'

'She really is unwell, I suppose?'

'We have to accept that she is, anyhow.'

'I'll have some flowers sent from the Society. With sympathy and best wishes for a speedy recovery. I think we should, don't you?'

'I suppose so. It would be a gesture.'

Somehow I was not enthusiastic. It seemed a bit overdoing the putting of a good face on it. Perhaps she really was unwell; but perhaps, also, when it came to it she felt that really it was too much to trek all the way across Ireland, East to West, to Galway. You could fly to Dublin from London, but then there was the long train journey. Perhaps she hadn't at first, when she accepted, realised that you couldn't fly all the way. Perhaps when it came to it the very thought of it made her feel unwell and tired. I know the feeling. And certainly Lakshmi Pandit wouldn't have realised how immensely important her visit had been to Galway, nor, therefore, how disastrous would be her cancellation.

But there it was, and the following evening I was one of the reception committee at the railway station to greet the Indian party, Rattan Bhalla and his wife from the embassy in Dublin, and Shivaramakrishnan, the handsome young press attaché from the High Commissioner's office in London, Her Excellency's representative.

Except that the charming Indian lady in the lovely sari was not Her Excellency, and that there was no military reception, everything was as planned. The party adjourned immediately to the hotel, without going outside the station, and the Bhallas, who were very nice, were conducted to their suite, and Madame's emissary to his bower. The management sent up champagne in a bucket of ice. I cannot remember, now, whether the Indians partook but I know that Joe and I did, feeling the need of it.

Next day there was luncheon in the hotel, for the Indian guests, the Society's committee members and their husbands and wives, and of course, Joe and myself. Before this there had been a reception in the hotel, with photographs taken, and an official welcome by the Chairman of the Committee, a charming young Irish Army officer, Captain Donal O'Donovan. After the luncheon Shivaramakrishnan, at his request, was taken for a drive, happy to have the opportunity of seeing something of the beauty of the West of Ireland. In the evening he and the Bhallas and I were collected at the hotel by taxi and driven to Mrs. Prendergast's house by a route that would take in the sights of Galway—the University, the Spanish Arch, the Claddagh, and Shivaramakrishnan was delighted to have seen the sun go down on Galway Bay, just as in the song. There was then the immaculate reception at Mrs. Prendergast's floodlit house in its floodlit garden, to the success of which the Bhallas, with their warmth and charm and diplomatic *savoir faire*, contributed enormously. Then back to the hotel in good time for the lecture at eight-thirty.

Exactly what the Galway Literary Society made of their young, handsome, charming Indian lecturer, with his exquisite poise, Joe O'Halloran and I feel we will never know, but undoubtedly he was something of a bombshell for the Galway intelligentsia, and undoubtedly he dropped, quite guilelessly, a

couple of medium-sized bombs. One was in reply to a question
from Colonel Cotton, at the end of the lecture, about Goa, the
Portuguese enclave in India, concerning which Pandit
Nehru's patience became exhausted in December, 1961, but
then it was still only October, 1960. The Colonel felt strongly
that Catholic Goa should remain Portuguese. But the so handsome, so charming, so altogether charismatic young press
attaché replied lightly, with his wonderful smile, 'Oh, Goa—
it is just a pimple on the face of India!' The Colonel who
also was very nice, was not amused.

The other bomb was somewhat heavier, for the speaker was
asked about India vis-à-vis Communist Russia—and in Catholic Ireland *Communist* is as dirty a word as in God's Own
Country, the United States of America. But equally lightly the
charming young man in whose name was embodied the whole
Hindu pantheon—or so it seemed, Shiva, Rama, Krishna—
replied, 'Our relations with the Soviet Union are excellent.'
Deep was the shudder that ran through the ranks of Tuscany
—in the person of the devoutly Catholic intelligentsia of Galway City. But such was the *charisma* of Her Excellency's
representative that at the end of the night his personality was
still exerting its charm. To this day, Joe tells me, when the
Old Hands of the Society meet they still recall, with a kind of
awe, that historic non-event, and the cool replies concerning
Goa, and the Soviet Union.

In the morning, when the Indian party was seen off on the
train for Dublin, everyone sent polite, sympathetic messages to
Her Excellency and trusted she would soon be better . . . for,
God between us and all harm, it might even have been true
that she was unwell, the creature.

3

Burmese Buddha via Ireland

When people come into my study for the first time they usually remark on a gilded Buddha image which fits into a corner of a stepped bookcase as though that niche had been specially made for it. The figure is about eighteen inches high, the classical image, seated in the lotus position, the right hand drooped over the right knee, the left lying palm upwards in the lap, the face fine-drawn and beautiful, in the Indian manner, the delicately modelled lips faintly smiling, the long eyes lowered in contemplation. Because the Lord Gautama was the Compassionate Buddha, who loved animals, I placed at the base of the image a tiny white kitten of Meissen porcelain; the kitten balances playfully on a gilded ball, and the effect of this delicate white and gold piece against the black painted block on which the Buddha sits is very pleasing. There is also, always, in all seasons, a small floral tribute in a little Japanese earthenware teapot at the base of the image. In Burma, from which this Buddha came, he would have been given jasmine and frangipani, fresh-gathered every morning, and glasses of water, and offerings of fruit. Here he is given whatever is available from the garden; in spring the small spring flowers, in summer a rose, later in the year a small hydrangea bloom, in winter a cluster of laurestinus leaves. I am not a Buddhist, yet, irrationally, it would somehow seem wrong if ever the little Japanese teapot held no offering.

People exclaim about the Buddha, which is very beautiful,

and tend to linger by it. Invariably I tell them the story.

I used this Buddha image in my Californian-background novel, *The Lady and the Mystic,* published in 1967, and it featured on the dust-cover, but only a garbled version of its history is told there, suiting the purpose of the narrative, and here I want to 'tell it like it was,' as the Americans say, and the true story is, in fact, stranger and more interesting.

When I returned from Burma in 1954 I wrote a book about my wanderings there, *Land of the Crested Lion.* The book was written at Oak Cottage and in Connemara between the spring and autumn of that year, and was published in 1955. I followed it with a Burmese novel, *The Living Lotus,* published the following year, and upon this book, also, I worked a good deal in Connemara. This novel was based on the case of the little Dutch girl who was left by her parents in Java during the Second World War and brought up by the Muslim family in whose care she was placed, married to a young Muslim school-teacher at the age of fourteen, and subsequently reclaimed by her Dutch parents, and, in the face of intense Indonesian opposition, brought back to Holland. This story entered very vividly into my imagination and I shared the Muslim indigna-tion at the uprooting of the girl from the environment in which she had grown up, and I wanted to write it, but I did not, then, know anything about the Muslim religion, and I did not know Indonesia, but by the time my interest was aroused in the story I did know a good deal both about Burma and Theravada Buddhism; the child in my story, therefore, was an Anglo-Burman little girl lost—not left—in Burma during the war and found and brought up by a Buddhist family, to be eventually traced and reclaimed by her English father and brought back to England. A great many Burmese religious customs and festivals are described in the novel, and, like the travel book, it produced a number of letters from Burma Old Hands—which was gratifying.

But the letter which led to my being given the Buddha was not from any Old Hand, but from an Irish woman, from County Clare, who had done war service in Burma—a good Catholic Irish woman. She wrote to me after reading *The Living Lotus,* which both she and her husband had much

Island View Cottage, Connemara

Shri and Shrimati Bhalla with Shivaramakrishnan at the Galway
Literary Society, 1960

The Burmese Buddha that came via Ireland

enjoyed, she said, and they had a Buddha image in their house, brought from Burma, and she would like to give it to me as an expression of gratitude for the pleasure she had had from what she was good enough to call my wonderful novel, but her husband had said I should have it after he was dead. Two years later I received the Buddha, which had been posted in England. The accompanying letter, with an English address, explained that the writer was the daughter of the Irish woman who had promised me the Buddha; her father having died, and she having been over in Ireland for the funeral, she had brought it back with her, at her mother's request, to send to me, in fulfilment of the promise.

In renewed correspondence with the mother I then learned the history of the Buddha image, which I recognised as typical of the Burmese Buddhist household shrine—I had seen such images in Burmese homes all over the country, loved and reverenced like the images of the Virgin in Irish Catholic homes. This one came from a village in the Meiktila province, south of Mandalay, in the Shan States, where I had spent some time, living with Burmese people in their homes, as I have described in *Land of the Crested Lion*. Meiktila, like Mandalay, is in the dry zone, which means that it is fearfully hot. The town of Meiktila stands on an artificial lake, which was traditionally created by the grandfather of Gautama Buddha, over two thousand years ago. That this very ordinary—though so beautiful—Buddha image came from this area, which is the most excitingly beautiful part of Burma, did of course enhance its interest and sentimental value for me.

The Japanese having over-ran Burma during World War II there was fierce fighting in this area when General Slim's army caught up with them, and in the 'battle of Meiktila' the Burmese fled from their villages—the owner of this particular Buddha image among them. She had kept her jewellery hidden in the base of the image, and when she fled she gave the Buddha, complete with the jewellery, to a Gurkha soldier to keep for her. When the Japanese were driven out the soldier faithfully returned the Buddha to its owner, with the jewellery intact, and in her gratitude she presented him with the image, as a memento. He accepted it, but as a Hindu had no use for it,

c

and when he learned of the Irish woman's interest in comparative religion he gave it to her, printing his name in ink in the bottom, with the date, S PRAKASH, in neat capitals, with the date below, 11.2.46—the date when she and her husband left Burma to return to Ireland, to County Clare—'so that I might remember him,' she wrote to me.

Sometimes I wonder about this Gurkha, and the Burmese woman who gave him the Buddha, and the Irish woman to whom he duly passed it on, and who after her husband's death had it sent to me from Ireland. I have never met her, but every Christmas she sends me a card, and I in turn send her greetings from the Meiktila Buddha . . . my most treasured material possession.

4

The Japanese Garden at the National Stud, Kildare

At this distance of time, some thirteen years later, I have forgotten who told me that there were some famous Japanese gardens in the Republic of Ireland, at a place called Tully, two miles from the town of Kildare, thirty miles or so from Dublin, but it would seem to have been someone in Japan, for it would appear from something I wrote at the time that ever since I got back from Japan in June, 1959, I had been planning to visit these gardens, and I did so in May the following year—just in time, as I wrote, to catch the last of the azaleas.

I still had the Connemara cottage at that time and was continually passing through Dublin, going and returning, sometimes spending a night there; with the Japanese gardens in mind I eventually resolved to spend two nights, and devote a day to the Tully expedition. This I did, and duly wrote an article about it, which for some reason was never used, and I reproduce it here :

At the hotel in Dublin they had never heard of the Japanese Gardens and gave me some misinformation about 'buses to Kildare. Aboard the wrong 'bus the conductor had never heard of Tully but brightened at the mention of the Japanese Gardens and knew they were near Kildare. He could also tell me which 'bus to take, and where from. He put me down opposite an entrance to Phoenix Park, where I discovered I had an hour to wait.

I wandered about the park, and because my mind was tuned in to Japan thought of Hibiya Park and Shiba Park in Tokyo, and, when a cold wind blew the litter about under the trees, of the *sekura*—cherry blossom—festival in Maruyama Park in Sapporo, where, under the blossoming trees, the litter is more than ankle-deep. By the time I boarded the right 'bus for Kildare I was already spiritually back in Japan.

When I descended from the 'bus at last in the sleepy little town of Kildare a taxi driver stepped forward from under a tree as though he had been expecting me, and sure he knew the Japanese Gardens—out at the National Stud, he said.

The two miles out to Tully seemed a long way—but then Irish miles are reputedly longer. I arranged with the taxi driver to return for me in an hour-and-a-half's time—it was a matter of getting the only 'bus back to Dublin from Kildare which would get me there in time for an evening appointment. The taxi driver assured me he'd be back on the dot of half-after-one, and drove off. I approached wrought-iron gates through which there was an exciting glimpse of a stone lantern, *ishi-doro*, which had an air of keeping guard among the trees. Excitement gave place to dismay when I read the notice by the gates which said in very plain English that the gardens did not open until two o'clock on Sundays—and it was a Sunday, and the taxi returning for me at half-past one.

Having got there I was determined to see the gardens even if I had to climb gates and scale walls to do so. I marched off in the direction of the stables of the National Stud and found a child who found a woman who found a man who proved to be the stud manager and the husband of the woman and the father of the child. To him I explained my predicament about the gardens, and how much it meant to me, having been in Japan, to see these gardens, and how I had stayed over in Dublin specially on my way back from the West, and how I had to go to England tomorrow, and who knew when I would be in Dublin again? He was a pleasant man and entirely sympathetic, as the Irish invariably are to a predicament, blessedly unaddicted to the official attitude, but explained that the difficulty was that there was no gardener available to take me round and explain things to me. I replied, eagerly, that I had no need of such a service, as I understood about Japanese gardens, having visited many in Japan. I wanted, I urged, only to be allowed to walk round and take a few photographs. . . .

At that point there arrived a man whom the manager seemed to have been expecting, from the greetings exchanged, and he had better things to do, it was clear, than argue the toss with this persistent English woman. He stepped into his office, took a key off a hook and a brochure from a rack, excused himself to the man who had come to see him about a horse, and commanded me to 'Come this way.'

I followed him to a small gate in a wall; he unlocked the gate and said that if I returned to the office when I was 'through' he would have me meet the head-gardener for a chat, if I cared to. The leaflet, he said, handing it to me, would explain the best way to tour the gardens and what they were all about. I should go all round and 'up the hill'.

I thanked him and pushed open the gate—and stepped into Japan.

The Japanese gardens at Tully—correctly, the Japanese Garden at the National Stud, Kildare—were devised by Lord Wavertree, and were made by a Japanese gardener called Eida, and his son, Minoru, in the years 1906 to 1910. The estate became government property, and the National Stud was established there, in 1949.

I was astonished to find in the brochure a poem in praise of the gardens by a woman poet, Helen Sevrez, I had known in my girlhood, in my advertising office days during World War I; I published some of her verses in *The Pelican*, of which I was in those years, in my teens, associate-editor with Charles (later Sir) Higham, my boss. After my first marriage, in 1920, I lost touch with her, and by the time I reached Kildare she had long been dead. Infinitely strange to me it seemed that all those years later I should be treading those paths she had trod . . . I wondered when, and wished I knew, and that she was still alive. I followed a narrow path flanked by bamboos and azaleas and pondered the mysterious orderings of human life in terms of *karma*. In the last forty years or so I had not thought about this friend of my youth; there had been no reason to; we had gone our separate ways; and then to meet again there seemed most strange. Only, of course, in terms of *karma* nothing is strange, but all an ordered pattern of continuity of conduct, of cause and effect. Her verses sound a Buddhistic note—'Here leads to Joy, the mystic path of Pain'—had she become a Buddhist, I wondered, or inclined to it, as I myself? I wished I knew. I wished I knew.

I turned from those troubling verses to the explanation of the gardens and learned that they were planned to symbolise the Life of Man, and the gateway through which I had passed was the Gateway of Oblivion, 'through which the Pilgrim Soul enters among the trees and passes into the open, where is a small cavern, the Cave of Birth, crowned by a cherry tree.' I passed through this small, fern-damp cave and came to a narrow winding path among rocks and boulders, symbolising the years of Childhood, 'unseeing and unknowing'. . . .

The brochure grandiloquently continues: '. . . we come to a mound of rock. Through this the tunnelled pathway leads from Darkness into Light; from Ignorance into the Unfolding of Knowledge. Half way through the winding tunnel is an opening, leading by stone steps to the Hill of Learning, crowned by an ancient fir tree. Often this fir-crowned height tempts the student to look too high, but there is an unguarded hole to teach him vigilance before he comes down the hill to the level of his fellows. Following a winding course, still guarded by rocks, he reaches the Parting of the Ways. On the right a forest of cherry blossom symbolises Temptation, and he who follows that path can never find the way to the Hill of Ambition. On the left is the straight path of Austere Living; in the centre the path of Wedded Life, by which the pilgrim reaches the tiny Island of Joy and Wonder, across the stepping-stones of Exploration. But he cannot stay there. All paths lead to further temptation across a stone bridge to the bamboo bridge and the Geisha House, but beyond them is the Hill of Ambition, and the Well of Wisdom is in sight, across the beautiful water. Very steep is the Hill, and those who climb may be separated, but as they climb they reach out helping hands, and are united at the top. Descending, the pilgrim finds an easy bridge across the roaring falls, and treads the stepping-stones through the level garden of Peace and Contentment to the Hill of Mourning, whence his soul goes forth through the Gate of Eternity.'

All of which is all very poetic, and highly misleading. Leaving all symbolism aside (and did Eida and Minoru really see their garden in these moral terms? Were they all that Zen? In my experience the common people of Japan are not. But perhaps Lord Wavertree was. Perhaps, even, he wrote all the allegorical stuff)—leaving all that symbolism aside, I was saying, the winding path from the entrance gate leads to an irregularly shaped lotus pond, across which an ancient tree trunk leans to form an archway to a wistaria-covered pergola. There are azaleas everywhere, and little flat-topped fir-trees among boulders, and little twisted pines in pots, and stone lanterns, old and gray, among small-leafed maples, and one by a hump-backed red-lacquered bridge over the lotus pool, and nearby is the tea-house, described in the brochure as a geisha house 'as authentic as any in Japan.' (Later, when I said to the head-gardener, whom I duly met when I returned to the office, that this was a tea-house, and by no means a geisha house, he replied that that was what a 'Japanese gentleman from the embassy in Dublin' had told him.)

I walked round the wooden verandah of the tea-house and felt myself back in the Kikokutei, the Abbot's garden in Kyōto designed by the famous poet, Ishikawa Jozan, in the early 17th century—very much this garden reminded me of that one, though this Irish one was very much better kept. It is, in fact, perfectly kept.

There are stepping-stones through streams, and across patches of lawn, and below the little hill—which is by no means steep—water cascades over boulders—hardly roaring falls—and there is a small stone Buddha image. A pine tree crowns the hill, but it is too tall and is quite un-Japanese, which is a pity. There are also too many flowers blooming amongst the rocks and boulders, detracting from the Japanese effect and offering too strong a suggestion of an English garden rockery.

But then the eye comes back to the red-lacquered hump-backed bridge, the weathered wood of the tea-house, the clean bare line of the tree trunk arching across the lotus stream to the wistaria pergola, and it could be the Kikokutei, or the wonderful garden behind the Heian shrine at Kyōto, which, with its backcloth of distant mountains is surely the most beautiful garden in the world. I certainly thought so at the time. That garden, too, I had blessedly to myself for as long as it took to explore its enchantments—then fled from it before an invading horde of school-children. Sunday 'bus loads would have invaded this garden at Tully, too, had I not left when I did, leaving behind them their carelessly discarded cigarette cartons and butt ends. (Is there comfort or despair in the thought that people are everywhere very much the same in the matter of litter, from Tokyo to Tully, from Kyōto to Kildare?) The head-gardener told me that the first thing he and his men did after every batch of visitors was to go round picking up the litter they had left. He said it without bitterness. Long years of experience had inured him to it, evidently.

I told him about the famous Zen garden, Ryōanji, in which there was not a shrub or tree or blade of grass, nothing but raked white sand and an arrangement of big boulders, and this he thought most wonderful, though he found it hard to understand why it should be called a *garden*. . . .

Some of the things growing in the gardens at Tully had been brought over from Japan fifty years ago, in Lord Wavertree's time, he said. In recent years they had been able to get suitable shrubs from a nursery near Dublin. He knew about *bonkei* —the tray landscapes we call here 'Japanese gardens'—and it was a great art, he said, but not easy to carry out here as it was difficult to get the right kind of plants and miniature shrubs necessary for it; the same with *bonsai*, the little dwarfed trees, though they had a few, in real Japanese porcelain pots, as I may have noticed. He understood that there were some Japanese gardens in England, and at Kew Gardens a fine avenue of Japanese cherry trees. I told him that this I had seen, and in spring it was very beautiful, but that it was not a piece of Japan set down in alien soil, such as this Japanese garden in Ireland. It would be fine if he could one day go to

Japan, I suggested. He smiled—the smile of a man who knows it will never happen.

Lord Wavertree, he said, liked to meditate in his Japanese garden. He would never make a decision about his horses without sitting first on the Hill of Learning and meditating.

I like to think his lordship meditated on other things than horses. Whether he did or not he devised for himself and posterity a small and exquisite thing of beauty, created by Japanese artist-gardeners, whose dream lives and flowers with the season, from the cherry blossom's ethereal loveliness, to the 'maples in flower', an alternation of beauty hidden away in that remote corner of the county Kildare, in the Republic of Ireland.

PART II

The Middle East

1

Down on the Gulf: Kuwait

Kuwait was not my introduction to the Gulf, as the Old
Hands call that five-hundred-mile stretch of water which the
world knows as the Persian Gulf, but which the Arabs insist on
calling the Arabian Gulf; I had been there earlier, from Basrah,
in the south of Iraq, and taken ten miles out into it to inspect
a floating dock built by the Basrah Petroleum Company so
that tankers can fill up there without having to journey up the
river at the head of the Gulf to Fao and Basrah; it was an
exhausting and ultimately tedious experience which I have
recorded in *A Lance for the Arabs.** I had finished with Iraq
and spent some time in Jordan, Syria, Lebanon, and was in
Cairo when I received the official invitation from the government to visit the State of Kuwait.

My first reaction had been to decline the invitation. I was
not much interested in this fabulously wealthy sheikdom whose
economy was entirely dependent on oil, and having been an
official guest so recently in Iraq, and General Qassim's attitude to Kuwait being, notoriously, what it was—an attitude
to which I was sympathetic—it seemed to me altogether not
'on'. But the envoy who brought me the invitation from the
Kuwait embassy in Cairo was a Palestinian; and he was very
nice; and he said, perceiving my hesitation, 'There are many
Palestinians in Kuwait ...'

I decided to accept, though had doubts as to whether I

* 1963.

would feel able to write about Kuwait, since along with not wishing to give offence to my hosts there was the problem represented by my loyalty to Abdel Karim Qassim, whom I had personally liked and in whose sincerity I believed. I went, and it was to prove quite as difficult as I had feared it might be, for I had an interview with the Ruler, Sheikh Abdullah Al-Salim Al-Sabah, who died in 1965, and all he wanted to talk about was my meeting with General Qassim. . . .

My 1962 mission in the Middle East was concluded with my visit to what was then the Gaza Strip, administered by Egypt, and *A Lance for the Arabs* ends with that chapter. I did, however, try to write something about Kuwait for a final chapter, and in fact wrote some four thousand words before abandoning it. I think now that I could have included at least some of this material in the book, without giving offence to the Kuwait government and I regret not doing so, for reading it after the interval of ten years it has, I think, a certain traveller's-tale interest, and offers a glimpse of the oily life down there on the Gulf. The following is extracted from it :

When Kuwait was founded in the 18th century by the Atabi Arabs, ruled by the Sabah tribe, it was a small desert town existing mainly by pearl-diving, fishing, and ship-building. At the outbreak of World War I it became a British Protectorate. Drilling for oil began in 1936, the Kuwait Oil Company being jointly owned by British and American companies, but owing to the intervention of World War II production did not get under way until ten years later, when in June, 1946, the then Ruler, Sheikh Sir Ahmad al Jabir al Sabah, turned a silver-handled valve to start the loading of a British tanker with the first cargo of crude oil. By then thirty thousand barrels per day were being produced. The boom had begun.

Sheikh Ahmad died in 1950 and was succeeded by his cousin, Sheikh Abdullah. All the members of the government, which is patriarchal, with the exception of three are sheikhs of the Sabah family, who ruled under the Turks. The income of the present ruler is reputedly four hundred million dollars a year, of which about one hundred and fifty million are invested in England, particularly in Treasury Bonds, annually. It is estimated that the total of these investments has now exceeded a billion dollars, so that if the Sheikh should inconsiderately withdraw his savings from this country . . . but His Highness would never do anything so unkind, because the British own half the oil concession in Kuwait, and he collects fifty per cent of the profits. The British are also his staunch defenders; his interests are theirs—and theirs are his. Well, obviously. The British share of the net profits of their concession is about two hundred and fifty million dollars a year.

All the Arab countries except one, Iraq, and the Arab League, recognise the independent status bestowed on Kuwait by the British in 1961. General Qassim's claim to Kuwait as an integral part of Iraq rested on the fact that since 1775, and until the First World War and the occupation of Iraq by the British, it was part of Basrah province. Under the Ottoman Sultan the rulers of Kuwait were subject to the Governor of Basrah. There are many official documents confirming this, and the interested reader is referred to J. G. Lorrimer's *Persian Gulf Gazetteer*, published in 1908.

Only a half, or less, of the population are Kuwaitis. The official figures as of May 21, 1961, were 321,621, of whom 161,909 were Kuwaitis, 30,990 Jordanians, with the figures for Palestinians given separately as 6,635; Iraqis 27,148. Michael Adams sent an article from Kuwait to the *Guardian* in December 1961 in which he gave the proportion of Kuwaitis as less than a third of the population.

When I asked, as I several times did, whether it was true that there are no poor people in Kuwait I was invariably told, 'There are no poor *Kuwaitis*.'

The pilot on the 'plane on which I flew from Cairo to Kuwait assured me I would find beggars in the streets. This I did not find, but in my wanderings around I did see people who were obviously poor, among the not yet demolished remains of the old town, down by the sea.

And in a housing leaflet I was given one of the three categories of 'People of Limited Income' is 'Destitutes'—defined as 'people whose monthly income is less than 19 Dinars'; that is to say less than £19 a month. For them houses are provided at a nominal rent of about 15/- per month per room. 'Distribution of the houses,' says the leaflet, 'is conducted by a

Committee of 11 members of Kuwaiti notables who are well-informed about the financial conditions of the various Kuwaiti families.'

(This, it will be remembered, was written in 1962; as I made no comment on it I can only assume that I did not, then, find it as ironically humorous as I do now.)

From this leaflet (continues the 1962 narrative) it would appear that *not* all Kuwaitis are prosperous, and certainly some of the *non*-Kuwaitis, notably the Palestinians, are doing well—in the oil companies, government employ, television and broadcasting, to name the three fields in which I found them.

With a high-up government official who was not a sheikh I found myself to my surprise discussing Kuwait in terms of the tragedy which had overtaken it—the flooding of this once small fishing village with oil, and therefore with money, which, said this remarkable official, 'has changed the character of the people'.

The pearling trade of the mid-18th century had already begun to decline before the mid-20th with the development of cultured pearls, but from 1946 the whole economy of Kuwait was based on the production of oil, and it was progress, progress all the way, with air-conditioning and modern blocks of flats and offices, and huge American cars for the shiny motor roads, and a vast modern hospital, and an enormous secondary school, and not anywhere near enough patients or pupils even to half fill either, and water distilled from the sea by a distillation plant said to be the biggest in the world, and brought to the houses in tankers and sold by the barrel (£1 a barrel at that time); and a new port costing 23 million dollars, and natural gas piped in from the oil fields, and electric power stations fuelled by this gas, and neon lighting, and the old houses round the old harbour and the market, with their walls fashioned from coral from the bay—all this going down and the high-rise buildings going up, and the general effect one of a quite frightening materialism and ugliness.

Then you begin to get used to it and notice that at least some of the modern building is quite handsome, and that trees have been planted everywhere and preposterous as it all is, this desert town became a sheikhdom, a patriarchal State, and producing

Kuwait: general view

Kuwait: the Secondary School

Author speaking in the open air at Qalqiya, on Jordan's West Bank,
April 1965

The black tents of the *bedu*

nothing but oil, you nevertheless begin to be interested. It is, after all, all very astonishing, to say the least.

My arrival at Kuwait airport was inauspicious—and eventually comic. The Kuwait embassy in Cairo had wired its Foreign Office in Kuwait the flight number and arrival time of my 'plane, but between the fact that the 'plane was delayed for two hours at Cairo, and that my married name seems somehow to have become involved in the booking, there was confusion at the Kuwait end; Foreign Office officials, and a television squad, had gone to the airport and met all the afternoon 'planes and then given it up. When I arrived around seven in the evening I was dismayed to find myself unmet. Whilst I was wondering what to do, having no idea what arrangements had been made for me, where I was to stay or who would be looking after me, a voice close to me said pleasantly, 'Good evening, Miss Mannin. I am from Mr. Bustani's office . . .'

[Emile Bustani, the Lebanese millionaire who crashed to his death in his private 'plane off the Beirut coast on a flight to Damascus, in March 1963, had been my host, and my very good friend in Beirut, and officials of his vast Contact and Trading Company, always known as C.A.T., had been of assistance to me everywhere in the Middle East.]

I did not know the C.A.T. man who found me in the crowd on Kuwait airport, and I do not know how he knew me. I am convinced that C.A.T. men have special gifts. Anyhow the young man from Emile Bustani's office got me rapidly through the Customs, and outside there waited a C.A.T. official I had met in Emile's office in Beirut, Mr. Mohammed Namani, the Resident Engineer of the C.A.T. camp in Kuwait. I was delighted—and much relieved—to see him, but too tired and confused to ask him how he knew the day and time of my arrival—or even that I was coming to Kuwait. So far as I am concerned C.A.T. works in a mysterious way its wonders to perform.

I was whisked off in a big shiny car to the C.A.T. camp, some way out of the town, beside a disused—or seldom used— palace. High walls surround both the palace and the compound of the camp, as though to keep out the encroaching

D

desert. In the camp compound are the pleasant bungalows of the C.A.T. employees; there are also offices, and 'Mr. Bustani's house.' I was taken to Mr. Namani's house and given a good meal and very welcome cold beer. Mr. Namani had discovered where I was to stay in the town and was about to take me there, after the meal, when a handsome young man from the Foreign Office turned up. In my tired and confused state he seemed, with his flowing white robes and streaming head-dress, and his dark good looks, like all the princes of Arabia rolled into one. I've no idea how he knew I was there in the C.A.T. camp. Perhaps Mr. Namani had done some telephoning. Perhaps, I thought, light-heartedly, there was some kind of bush-telegraph in that hot little artificial oasis at the edge of the desert. He was anyhow obviously relieved to have found me—and asked if I would mind returning to the airport with him in order to be shown on television officially arriving. . . .

It was a little embarrassing, and it seemed absurd, but if that is what they wanted—

So back I went in an enormous Foreign Office car and at the airport a television crew waited and I was televised entering the V.I.P. lounge, half as big as the Albert Hall ('It is for the Ruler when he travels,' it was explained to me) and photographed from all angles sitting in it. Mr. Namani, who had come with us in his own car, carefully detached himself from the proceedings. On the wall behind where I sat was a larger than life-size portrait of the Ruler, regally robed.

This bit of play-acting over I was driven back into town—to be photographed coming up the steps of the hotel, its entrance flanked by potted plants. The interior of the hotel had a kind of suburban splendour of pink brocade curtains and pink satin bedspread and ultra-modern lighting. Downstairs, in the lounge, there were meaningless modern mural decorations and people sitting about drinking soft drinks—because, as the 'plane pilot had warned me, Kuwait is 'dry'. That is to say, no alcohol is available in hotels and there are no bars, but clubs are licensed, and for home consumption there is a ration —it presented no problem, Mr. Namani declared, in reply to my anxious inquiry, and presented me with a bottle of brandy, discreet in a small suitcase, in token thereof; together with the assurance that more would be forthcoming if required.

(In fact, Dr. Saba George Shiber, a Christian Palestinian whom I had the pleasure of knowing in Kuwait, and who died suddenly in 1968 in his early forties, wrote in an article on Arab Cities which appeared in English in the *Middle East Business Digest* in October, 1967, that 'even though prohibition is the law of the land, more liquor is said to be drunk here per head than in any Arab city.' In the same article he wrote, also, 'Though a dry State by law, Kuwait manages to live up to its reputation of being quite wet, and one rarely experiences a non-existence of alcohol wherever he happens to be at night,' adding, 'How this is the case defies the imagination and explanation of this author.' George Shiber, whom I liked very much, was the son-in-law of Dr. Izzat Tannous, my oldest living Palestinian friend, brought to Oak Cottage in the thirties by Reginald, and whom I was to meet again in the Middle East in the sixties. One of the displaced and dispossessed of 1948 he lives now in Beirut.)

My escort in Kuwait was the charming young man attached to the Foreign Office; he was American-educated and intended to return to the U.S.A. for the completion of his studies and to make some branch of the diplomatic service his career. He was a Kuwaiti and very enthusiastic about his country's progress and its extensive social services, and keen to show me all possible in the few days at my disposal. Like all Kuwaitis he wore the national dress, the flowing robes and the headdress fastened by a black cord.

That a great deal is being done in Kuwait, socially and educationally, is indisputable. There is every reason why it should be, with such vast wealth at its disposal and so small a population. It is claimed that in Kuwait an ideal community is being established in the Arab world, with equality of opportunity and a high standard of living.

(George Shiber wrote in 1966, '. . . what is beyond the least shadow of doubt is that the person ensconced in Kuwait or in a post in Kuwait, enjoys a higher standard of physical living than exists in any other Arab city. A villa here is like a palace elsewhere, a low-income house costs as much as a villa in, say, Amman or Jerusalem. People have big cars, expensive furniture, TV sets, expensive clothes, enjoy free medical care and education, and salaries are higher than in any other Arab city.')

Kuwait is undeniably progressive—intensively so; almost overwhelmingly so. For the vast secondary school, almost a town in itself, and the nucleus of the university, are both virtually empty; there just are not enough people to fill them—as with the vast Sabah hospital, with its 800 beds. There are 112 schools in Kuwait, apart from the enormous secondary school and the kindergartens; there are 13 hospitals and dispensaries. And the number of cars is estimated as a sixth of the population. It is not a big population but it is a lot of cars. It is not quite true that everyone has a Cadillac, as I had been assured before I set out, but there are a good many about, and there are Cadillac taxis. And they say that nobody bothers with a secondhand car; when you feel you have had your car long enough you just drive it out into the desert and buy another. That, I think, is one of the likelier stories, for the desert is littered with dead cars.

There were things I liked in Kuwait, and chief among them was the excessive tree-planting zeal. There are about 70,000 trees planted out by the Sabah hospital, between it and the sea, so that in time the hospital will overlook a virtual forest. There are main streets with young trees down the middle, and a side street going down to the sea has been planted with ornamental palms; there are, too, streets flanked by the dusty-looking, pine-like athal trees, which anyhow provide a little shade. I liked the public gardens in the centre of the city, with pools and shelters, and I tremendously admired the faith and courage of all this horticultural effort in this desert place.

I was driven out into the desert to a children's holiday camp. They were illegitimate and abandoned children from a home in the town, brought out there to camp in tents 'for a change'. A hot high wind was blowing the sand unpleasantly, and the place was black with flies. An ice-cream van had just come out from the town, and the children's hands and mouths were sticky with the ice-cream, attracting the flies, which clung undisturbed even by the children's movements, the way they persist round the eyes and mouths of animals.

Flapping futilely at the flies myself I suggested to the nice youngish woman in charge of the thirty-three children that it might have been better to have had the camp by the sea—there were so many flies here, and the wind blowing the sand . . .

She agreed that the flies and the sand were a nuisance but declared that it would be dangerous to take the children to the sea. (I learned later that the sea is shallow for a hundred metres out.) Some of the little girls were wearing velvet dresses, very pretty, but singularly inappropriate in that place and in that heat. It was difficult to see what the children did out there in the desert that they couldn't have done better on the grass and under the trees of the very beautiful gardens of the secondary school—where nobody ever goes.

I was taken, also, to a dusty stretch of coast to which people drive at weekends to picnic. There are a few scrawny pine trees here offering a thin shade, but you have to get there early to secure a tree, for they soon get booked up, those growing on low ridges being particularly popular for some reason. The sea is quite a way off, but no one bothers with it anyhow. The drill is that when you have secured a tree you park your car and bring out rugs and strips of carpet to sit on, and material for starting a fire, for a picnic means a shish-kebab, washed down by canned beer, the cans to be left lying. The whole dusty area is littered with cans and orange peel and ice-cream cartons; the desert will absorb them all in time, of course, but it takes time. The sea when you get to it is inaccessible; there is a lot of barbed wire, and mounds of earth; perhaps when the new corniche is made it will be better; and I am assured there are accessible beaches, good ones.

I liked the big wooden sailing barges, the *dhows*, lying down by the old harbour, with its stone walls; some of them bring produce from Iran; others are relics of the old pearling and fishing days. There is a very fine big wooden ship, an old pearl-fishing *dhow*, in dry dock beside the square clock tower facing the secondary school gardens—kept as a relic of the past, like the *Cutty Sark* by the Thames at Greenwich.

I was taken to a Vocational Training Centre for the handi-capped, where I saw furniture and basket work made by the blind, and some good leather and needlework and woodwork done by maladjusted people and partially crippled people. The people live at home but come to the centre for training. There is a section where senile old men and women, and mild mental cases, are cared for. The rooms all stood open on to long cor-ridors in which burning joss-sticks sweetened the air. It was anyhow better than the carbolic which characterises Western institutions. The building stands in a lovely flower garden but no one seemed to want to walk or sit out in it.

I returned later in the day for a Mothers' Day celebration. The gardens then were gay with coloured paper chains rattling in the hot high wind. It was an occasion for mothers and child-ren only, and a large square was packed with black-wrapped women and lively children. In the middle of the square, in a bandstand, musicians banged on drums and played various in-struments, but no one listened. There was a great deal of stand-ing on chairs. Eventually some kind of game to do with numbers was organised by a man speaking through a micro-phone and children wandered about with tickets looking for matching numbers. There was a table laden with prizes—dolls and plastic toys and boxes of chocolates, flower vases, and so forth.

I was taken, also, to a girls' secondary school, large and handsome and modern, and to a school for deaf-and-dumb and blind children which is to be rebuilt because it is not large and handsome and modern enough.

There is still something of the old brown city of Kuwait left, with its alleyways and its mud walls, but anyone wanting to see it will have to hurry, for it is being demolished fast. The corniche will extend along the entire waterfront and sweep away the old market, which is to be moved to outside the town. It is considered that the old city is not worth preserving—whether the life that went with it is, is another matter. 'It is the price we pay for progress,' said my young man, approvingly.

One morning early when I was wandering along the water-front looking at the *dhows* and the green scum in the old stone-walled harbour, which made it look like an Irish field, there were long blasts on a shrill motor horn and turning I saw a retinue of cars, those fore and aft open, and scarlet-clad figures standing up in them—it was the Ruler passing from his residential palace to the one in which he rules.

'You must meet the Ruler,' I was told.

'Oh dear!' I said, alarmed.

But then I thought that he was after all only one more Arab, only richer than the others.

The Chamberlain who conducted me to the Ruler, putting a brown robe on over his white one before he did so, spoke perfect English and had the gift of rapid translation. I was so blinded by television lights as I entered the room in which His Highness waited that it was a moment before I realised that he was not facing me as I expected but seated in a corner by the door, on the left, as I stumbled blindly in, and I had to swing round to confront him, awkwardly.

I apologised and explained as we shook hands, and this was quickly translated, and the reply, 'His Highness says that we all make mistakes and television is one of them, but it is something we have to put up with.'

It was indicated that I should be seated. The Chamberlain remained standing, but after a few formal, polite questions and answers had shuttlecocked to and fro the Ruler motioned to him, too, to be seated.

There then proceeded an interrogation, and I felt as though I was in the witness box :

'His Highness asks if you met General Qassim when you were in Baghdad.' (He, of course, knew damn well I did.)

'I had that honour.'

'His Highness would be interested to know what you thought of him.'

My reply was a model of diplomacy.

'I thought him a man of great personal charm.'

I was well aware that the Ruler of Kuwait would not be in the least interested in the charm of the Prime Minister of Iraq, but it was, in the circumstances, an unfair question. The same question was put to me later in a television interview and I gave the same reply—having warned the Palestinian who was conducting the interview to 'leave Qassim out of it,' because I wasn't going to play.

That the Ruler of Kuwait should feel anything but bitter about Qassim, his territorial claims and his threatened invasion, was to be expected; yet Qassim had reason for bitterness too, and though we had discussed Kuwait in the long late-night talk I had had with him in Baghdad he had said nothing personal about the Ruler. The Sheikh sat with his feet drawn up into his chair and I sat looking at his beige-coloured slippers whilst I listened, respectfully, to his explanation of the falsity of Iraq's claims to Kuwait, General Qassim's 'falsification of history' in that respect, coupled with an indictment of his personal and political character. But I knew it all; I had been given official, Government of Kuwait, publications about it— *The Truth about the Crisis between Kuwait and Iraq*, and *The Kuwaiti-Iraqi Crisis*, in which Qassim was likened to Hitler and Mussolini, and his rule declared to be 'nothing but disasters and massacres'. I knew all that, but then there was nothing to do but sit, patiently, politely, regarding the points of the beige slippers and wait for an opportunity to change the subject. There was something I had been resolved to tell this fabulously rich sheikh if I met him, and that was about the T.B. hospital in Gaza, and the distressed and angry Egyptian doctor who was throwing in his hand in despair, since he lacked the essential drugs and equipment, and there were not even proper arrangements for the washing of the clothes and sheets of the patients, and when he asked U.N.W.R.A. for anything he was always told that funds were not available, that something called 'the budget' would not permit of any more being spent on the hospital.

I seized the opportunity when His Highness came to the end of his indictment of Abdel Karim Qassim, and the conversation flagged, to say that I had recently been in Gaza and was worried about the T.B. hospital, which, I said, was a miserable place from lack of funds to provide the necessary drugs and equipment, and U.N.W.R.A. had said it could do no more.

'There is not even a washing-machine !' I said, boldly.

After all, what is a washing-machine when your income is

four hundred million dollars a year? Not that a single washing-machine would have solved the problem of the hospital's
unhygienic handling of the patients' laundry, but it was a useful symbol of the hospital's urgent need.

'I feel,' I continued, recklessly, with a fine disregard for
protocol, 'that a rich country like Kuwait should be able to
subsidise a small hospital like this—put it on its feet.'

I wondered, afterwards, how that went into Arabic, but anyhow the answer came back in the Chamberlain's immaculate
English that His Highness wished to assure me that the Arab
countries did everything possible for the refugees, wherever
they were.

I suppose I should have pointed out that the patients in the
Gaza T.B. hospital were not necessarily refugees; there were
still Gaza Palestinians, *al-hamdu lillah,* God be praised, outside
the camps, but, weakly, perhaps, I felt I had been over-bold
already. Later, back in Beirut, I wrote to the Minister of
Health in Kuwait about various matters and mentioned this
hospital and my concern for it. I received the classic reply :
'This matter will, no doubt, be referred to the competent
authorities.' I did not answer the letter. What was the use?
The 'competent authorities' were U.N.W.R.A., who had said
they could do no more; and I was not in any case discussing
the competent authorities; I was asking *Kuwait* for help.

The interview with the Ruler took place in the Official
Palace, which is by the sea. The ceiling of his office—if the long
narrow room in which he sat by his desk is that—is composed
of panels depicting glamorous Western-style females. The ceiling is very famous. So are the mirror-topped tables which
reflect the ladies, so that whether you look up or down you are
regaled by the sight of feminine charms. I asked about the
ceiling—'Who are all these lovely ladies?' I received the unlikely reply, 'English queens.' The Chamberlain explained that
the ceiling had been so designed to please the Bedouin chiefs
when they were guests of the Sheikh, and who believed that
at night the ladies would come down from the ceiling and
dance for them. . . .

At the end of the interview, which I suppose lasted an hour
or less, the Chamberlain showed me something of the palace,

about which there was nothing noteworthy, except, perhaps, a handsome reception room hung with yellow velvet curtains. Across from this old palace a new palace is being built and I was shown something of this, too. It was designed to blend with the old one, the Chamberlain explained, and will look out over lagoons to be created from the old stone-walled harbour where at present the *dhows* lie.

It would have been impolite to ask whether His Highness really *needed* another palace, so there was nothing to do but murmur, 'That will be nice. . . .'

The 1962 narrative ends there. At that point I realised that I was not going to include a chapter on Kuwait in *A Lance for the Arabs*, that it was too 'tricky', and therefore no purpose served in continuing to write the story of the Kuwait visit—though I wish, now, that I had, if only for the record. It seems to me quite extraordinary that I did not complete the report. Was I that much besotted with Qassim and Iraq that I could just throw away the Kuwait experience? Well, it would seem so; with the result that now, ten years later, I must rely on memory for the rest of the story.

But there are only two other things of interest to record. One is tea at the palace of a Government Minister—a sheikh of the Sabah family. He had two palaces; this one was his summer palace, by the sea; whether he was in residence there I do not know, for it was not then summer but early spring. This sheikh was being subjected to criticism at the time for his plurality of marriages, and was under some pressure to abandon the idea of—I believe—his thirteenth. One of his latest wives had been a German woman, but she had by then been pensioned-off and was living in a villa in Beirut—which must surely have been more *gemütlich* than any palace-by-the-sea in Kuwait. Be that as it may . . . I was invited to tea there, with Emile Bustani's daughter and her husband who were then in Kuwait and staying at the Bustani house at the C.A.T. camp. So we drove to the Sheikh's summer residence 'and it will be interesting for you,' they said.

It was a pleasant palace, rather like the one I had recently

visited, the Sief Palace, for my interview with the Ruler; this
one, also, stood by the brilliant blue waters of the Gulf; there
were Moorish arches, and it was cool inside with tiled floors
and walls. To take tea we perched on brocaded and gilded
settees in an enormous drawing-room, and tea was served by
several men servants, one to hand the sandwiches, another the
cakes, and so forth. After tea our host, regal as the Ruler himself, with his white robes and flowing head-dress, conducted us
through the hot open spaces of the palace grounds—I remember flower beds multi-coloured with cosmos—to a large pool,
in the middle of which was a fountain; at a word of command
to one of the several gardeners hovering in the background a
switch was turned on somewhere and the fountain gushed high
in the air, changing colour as it fell, and all over the gardens
smaller fountains spurted in different colours. It somehow just
made the hot afternoon seem hotter—all these colours. No
doubt it was better at night.

The other Kuwait memory is a visit to the small island of
Failaka, which I wanted to see simply because it was there
and I was curious about it, and have anyhow a liking for small
islands.

'I would like to visit the island,' I said.

My hosts immediately raised objections.

'You cannot go there,' they said. 'There are no lunches.'

I replied, cheerfully, that I didn't mind about lunch; we
could take sandwiches. This produced general confusion,
which was finally sorted out—for *lunches* read *launches,*
throughout.

Frivolously, then, I said, 'If there are no boats couldn't you
lay on a helicopter?'

To my astonishment they did; a military helicopter.

It was my first, and, to date, only experience of this form of
transport. I found it an interesting rather than a pleasurable
experience. Climbing up over the huge wheels to get into the
machine reminded me of climbing elephants in India. Once in
you sit three or four aside, facing each other, in a kind of small
cab; when the doors are open at the sides you have a fine view,
but also the feeling that it would be very easy to fall out. The
noise is deafening. But a helicopter is undoubtedly very handy;

it can go where more sophisticated machines cannot; like the elephant in the Indian jungles it makes the inaccessible accessible.

The helicopter which made Failaka accessible for me took off from the military airfield of Kuwait; my companions were my Foreign Office escort, of course, Dr. George Shiber, and a young Army officer. It was a very short trip—the journey took about fifteen minutes—the island being only some thirty-five kilometres off shore. I had been warned that there was 'nothing really to see there', though there had in fact been Danish archaeological expeditions to the island, uncovering Greek temples, which unfortunately I didn't know at the time. But whether there was anything to see or not I didn't want to leave Kuwait without visiting the off-shore island. For one thing it is inhabited, and the last of the old Kuwait life goes on there in its small fishing community—that is something I would have liked to have investigated.

White-robed figures came running as the helicopter landed, both men and women, and there was a scampering of children; it would have been interesting to have seen their village and the school and clinic, but I was whisked off to see all-there-was-to-see, which proved to be a small archaeological museum, of the contents of which I remember nothing at all.

What I remember of the museum of Failaka—and, for those interested in such things, the island's civilisation dates back to the 4th century B.C.—is that a small bird had flown in with us, and when I left was fluttering up and down a window, and that I was concerned and agitated to get it out.

When I expressed this concern there was a certain amount of flapping about to that end, until the young man from the Foreign Office said firmly, 'Miss Mannin, it is well known that this is a very stupid kind of bird, and if we are to get it out we shall be here all day, and we must return to Kuwait and continue with your schedule. *Y'allah!* Let us go.

Like the old man in the shuttered house in *The Cherry Orchard*, after the family had left, I thought miserably, as we walked back to the helicopter.

.   .   .

The Government has a plan to develop Failaka as a tourist resort, with 'a modern port to receive ships and big launches, a large corniche to circle the coastal areas for the development of beaches and other tourist attractions, the building of casinos on the coastal strips.' It is also planned to 'revive the historical sites at Failaka island. In addition a new hotel is expected to be built to receive Kuwaitis and foreign visitors. Besides internal new roads Failaka will be linked with the Kuwaiti mainland through fast and large launches which will run on an organised schedule.'

2

Making a Film with the Arabs

Perhaps distance does sometimes lend enchantment to the view, but when it fails to do so it can sometimes lend a wry humour, so that what at the time was frustrating and nervously exhausting, and finally, perhaps, plain tiresome, can come to seem comic—in a down-beat sort of way.

Or so it seems to me, looking back to the hectic, exasperating, and exhausting twelve months between April 1964 and April 1965 I spent to-ing and fro-ing between Cairo and Amman making-a-film-with-the-Arabs. Trying, that is to say, to get the project of an Egyptian-Jordanian film of my Palestine novel, *The Road to Beersheba*, off the ground. In 1965 I was in Cairo four times and Amman twice between mid-February and mid-April, with a final visit to Amman in July—when I declined to return to London via Cairo. When I returned to London from Cairo in May, 1964, three days later I flew to Washington D.C., which was also a strictly Arab occasion, to celebrate the publication of the novel in U.S.A., a reception being given for the author by the Kuwait embassy, the then ambassador being himself a Palestinian.

The idea of making a film of this novel originated with an Egyptian lawyer, Adel Amin, living and working in Cairo, whom I first met in Cairo early in 1962 and came to know better when I was there again in the autumn of 1963. The novel was published in England late in November, by which time I was back in London. Designed as an 'answer' to the best-selling Zionist novel, *Exodus*, this novel, which set forth part of the story of the *other* exodus—the enforced exodus of a million Palestinian Arabs in 1948, following the creation of the Zionist state of 'Israel', at the heart of the Palestinian homeland—made a considerable impact on the Arab world. It was immediately done into Arabic in both Cairo and Amman; it was serialised in a Jordanian newspaper, and given in about thirty instalments on Radio Cairo. (I owe it to myself, perhaps, to mention here that I received no money for any of this; I was not even consulted; but that is all right; mine was the honour...)

Adel Amin read the book in English and was convinced that it would make a film, and that it *should* be made, as a counter-blast to Zionist propaganda. He wrote me, full of enthusiasm, to London. I replied a good deal less enthusiastically; I said, in effect, that it was a nice idea that there should be a film stating the Palestine Arab case, and if my novel should serve the purpose that was entirely 'O.K. by me', only—if the film was made, where would it be shown? There was no point in making it merely to show it in the Arab countries, I pointed out; it would only be worthwhile if it were shown in the West—to let in some light on the Palestine tragedy of an entire nation displaced and dispossessed, with almost a million Palestinians rotting in camps in Jordan, Syria, Lebanon; but since the film industry in the West was mainly in Jewish hands how was it proposed to get the film distributed? The objection was swept aside; the film industry was not entirely Jewish-con-trolled; in England, for example, there was the Rank organisation, and there were the Italians—there was Fellini. One way or another the film would be distributed in Europe and the U.S.A. It would be made by the Egyptians, who had a film industry, unlike the Jordanians, but the film would of course be shot in Jordan, where the main action of the story took place. What was of immediate importance was to secure the interest and co-operation of the Egyptian Minister of Information—then Dr. Hatim—and the services of an Egyp-tian film distributor—and who better than Fathi Ibrahim, head of a nationalised film industry? When next I came to Cairo we would work together on the script; meanwhile he and

a group of friends had formed a company for making the film
—one of them was an experienced film camera-man—and they
were calling themselves the Arabic Bureau for Cinema, and as
such they would treat with Dr. Hatim and Fathi Ibrahim.
There would, Adel declared, confidently, be money in it for all
of us; quite a lot of money. I liked Adel and I trusted him
implicitly; the Egyptians did make films, though by all
accounts not very good ones, and I supposed they could make a
film of *The Road to Beersheba,* given the co-operation of the
Jordanians, which, I also supposed, would not be with-held.
But I could not overcome my feeling that even if the film were
made, and competently made, it would not, could not, be
distributed in the West effectively, if at all, and would thus be
a waste of time, effort, and money.

But Adel and his friends thought otherwise, and in the face
of their insistence and enthusiasm I capitulated and played
along with them and tried to believe in it all. In April and May
of 1964, in Cairo, the discussions about the film seemed endless; there were meetings of the A.B.C. company at Adel's
apartment in Garden City, close to the Nile and across the
road from the two big hotels, Shepheard's and the Semiramis;
there were late-night discussions in the Night and Day café of
the Semiramis; there were discussions at my hotel, the old
Continental, facing across the square to the Opera House, with
the slightly sinister desert Moqqatim hills behind; there were
discussions over morning coffee at Groppi's, and over evening
drinks in the bar of the *Omar Khayyám* ship moored in the
Nile.

When I got back to London after the Washington interlude
that spring there was the Nubian novel, *The Burning Bush,**
to write, and the proofs of *Aspects of Egypt†* to deal with, and
I was not in the Middle East again until October, when I
flew to Amman as the guest of the Jordanian Ministry of
Information—a visit organised by the then Jordanian ambassador in Washington, with the object of collecting material for
a book about Jordan.‡ In my correspondence with Adel Amin

* 1965.
† 1964.
‡ *The Lovely Land,* 1965.

it had been agreed that I should discuss the film project with Salah Abu Zeid, the Jordanian Minister of Information, who was already in touch with the Minister in Cairo, Dr. Hatim.

On that visit to Amman I met King Hussein for the first time; I had had the honour to be in the convoy which accompanied him on his tour of the north. I was formally presented to him by Abu Zeid when we arrived at the village of Jeftleck, but when we were leaving the King detached himself from the group of ministers and officials and came over to me and said, 'You are very welcome in my country,' and when I thanked him added, 'You must come often!' I replied that if we made the film of *The Road to Beersheba* I would have occasion to, and he declared, vehemently, 'We shall make it!' I told this story in my book about Jordan, *The Lovely Land,* but repeat it here as part of the saga of making-a-film-with-the-Arabs.

What I did not record in *The Lovely Land* was that on the evening of the day I got back from the tour with the King there turned up, newly arrived from Beirut, a lively and engaging—and conceited—Palestinian called Ali Siam. I had previously met him in Kuwait, in 1962, when he interviewed me for a radio programme—and tried hard to make me talk about General Qassim, whom I had recently met in Baghdad and who was threatening to annex Kuwait. He was good-looking and intelligent, and I had liked him well enough to be pleased to meet him again in Amman. But my pleasure was to prove short-lived, for when he came to the hotel that evening and we talked, inevitably, of the film, he declared, emphatically, that it would not be made by the Egyptians. It had to be made, he insisted, by Europeans, who had the know-how, with a first-class script-writer, and a famous producer such as the Italian Fellini, or the Lebanese Kazan. It had to be taken out of Egyptian hands, and the initiative for this would rest with the Jordanian government. I protested that it had already been announced as a joint Egyptian-Jordanian project; King Hussein had himself announced it in those terms from Jerusalem, and the announcement had received wide publicity—and acclaim—in both Jordan and Egypt. Ali Siam swept this aside, impatiently—all that had merely been at the outset; now that the project began to be a reality the situation

E

was changed; we would discuss it with Abu Zeid. I felt worried and upset; the project was Adel Amin's, and with the formation of the ABC company he had put a lot of work into it; how could it now be wrested from him—either legally or morally? Egyptians were not to be trusted, Ali declared, airing a prejudice. It was absurd, and it was tiresome, but also distressing.

We went together to see the Minister the following afternoon at the Ministry of Information—just up the road from the hotel. The conversation at least clarified the situation from the Jordanian point of view; Abu Zeid was firm that the film would be made strictly at government level, Jordanian-Egyptian, and that there was no place in it for this ABC film company, or any other Egyptian concern. Adel Amin was out —and Ali Siam was in. I was to take a letter from Abu Zeid to Dr. Hatim confirming that the film was to be made at governmental level and that he would be sending someone to Cairo to discuss it. (This, in fact, was to prove unacceptable; understandably, Dr. Hatim, as Minister of Information, was not prepared to treat with anyone less than his Jordanian opposite number.) What had to be discussed, between the Jordanian and Egyptian ministries was who was to make the film; certainly not any Egyptian company, as the Jordanians —in the person of Abu Zeid and Ali Siam—saw it. I recorded, exhaustedly, in my journal: 'Ali Siam has taken over. I suspect it's for the good of the film, but I wonder what Adel's reactions will be.'

Later that day I recorded: 'Ali Siam irritates me with the nonsense he perpetually talks about England. If it goes on I shall probably lose my temper.'

Clearly, under the strain of the worry about the film the young man was beginning to get on my nerves. But the following day there was a dinner party given in Jerusalem in my honour, and Ali was among the guests. I recorded: 'Ali was in good form and laughing a lot—he has an infectious laugh, and, when he likes, a warmth of manner which makes one forgive him. But I still think he is, as I told him, spoilt and conceited, and, what I didn't tell him, fundamentally hard. He is "taking over" the film, and I am worried about Adel.' But there would seems to be no doubt that, *malgré tout*, he had charisma, this Ali Siam.

A few days later I flew to Cairo. I had looked forward to meeting Adel Amin and his friends again, but now I dreaded it. As an emissary to Jordan for the Egyptian end of the film project I had proved singularly unsuccessful, having to all intents and purposes capitulated to the Jordanians.

(It has some relevance here, I think, to mention that in general the Jordanians and Egyptians do not like each other very much. The Egyptians tend to regard the Jordanians as 'backward', lacking in the Western know-how, and therefore inferior; the Jordanians—and here I include Palestinians, who in Jordan have Jordanian nationality—tend to regard the Egyptians as not really Arabs, which in fact they are not, *pace* the late President Nasser's passionate pan-Arabism, and many Egyptians, Adel Amin among them, also declare that they are not Arabs. The Arabs are Semites, they say, and so they are. But what the Egyptians really are is as difficult to determine as what a Briton really is. And I would here refer the interested reader to a valuable book by the distinguished American anthropologist, Dr. Ashley Montagu, *Man's Most Dangerous Myth: the Fallacy of Race,** which converted me to the idea he so strongly maintains that the word 'race' should be eliminated from the language, as fundamentally meaningless.)

I was to be in Cairo this time not as an official guest, as hitherto, but as the guest of the Arabic Bureau of Cinema, and Adel Amin had booked me into the Semiramis hotel, conveniently close to his apartment.

I found on my arrival that no appointment had been made for me to see Dr. Hatim, and his righthand man told me on the telephone that it would be more immediately useful to see Fathi Ibrahim. I recorded wearily in my journal, 'I can't get the hang of all these film involvements.'

To my intense relief Adel was singularly undisturbed by the Jordanian attitude and the Ali Siam take-over. He dismissed as nonsense that the Arabic Bureau for Cinema had no place

* Published by Meridian Books, The World Publishing Company, U.S.A., 4th edition enlarged and revised, 1965.

in the making of the film, which was *their* project, whatever the Jordanians, in the person of the Ministry of Information and this Ali Siam, who ever he might be, might state to the contrary. If the Jordanians wanted to go ahead with a film of their own let them, but Hussein had given his blessing to the joint project. The thing now was to get the contract between me and the ABC drawn up, signed, and witnessed, before we went along to see Fathi Ibrahim.

Not that it worked out anything like so efficiently, for the morning after I got back to Cairo Adel and I went out to spend the day at his brother's orange groves in the country, some miles out of the city, and at the hotel in the evening I ran into the Jordanian Minister of Health, whom I had known in Jerusalem and liked very much, and we were joined by the Jordanian ambassador, whom I also liked very much—and whom I had to see in connection with the film, anyhow—as a result of which pleasant encounters Adel and I arrived late at the garish offices of Mr. Fathi Ibrahim. He proved to be fat and friendly and 'American', and he received us cordially enough, but the interview really amounted to nothing, because all Mr. Ibrahim had to say was that he 'agreed in principle' about the film but had to show the documents we took to him —which Adel took, that is to say, and I have no idea what they were—to the board, and when the board had examined them we should meet again. A good deal of the conversation was in Arabic, though Mr. Ibrahim—like Adel—spoke very good English.

After that Adel and I adjourned to the roof bar of the Hilton and drank cold beers and talked. Adel seemed to think the interview with Fathi Ibrahim satisfactory, and I had given up attempting to understand anything. From the Hilton, feeling rich—we were after all in the film business!—we taxied to the office of Adel's lawyer friend, where I duly signed the contract. We then went to Night and Day with a judge friend of Adel's, who had turned up, and drank brandy to celebrate the signing of the contract. All we had to do now, apparently, was to make the film.

The producer was a pleasant young Egyptian, Abdel Khader Telmissany, one of the ABC group, who was 'in films'. I had

met him when last in Cairo, in April, and we saw him the day
after the signing of the contract. I wrote in my journal:
'Whether he can really handle so big a production I don't
know. He admits to being afraid of it, but I suppose that is
nothing against him.' We met him again next day and drafted
a telegram to Abu Zeid asking for some action on the Jordanian part of the contract. The journal records: 'The wire was
not as explicit as Telmissany and I wished, but Adel was
adamant. I wanted to ask Abu Zeid to wire as to whom he was
sending here to treat with Dr. Hatim, and when. I also pointed
out to Adel that the Jordanians can't sign anything when they
haven't—as yet—anything to sign! After some argument Adel
agreed to draft a contract next day.'

After sending the wire we went to the office of Adel's lawyer
friend, where we met another of the ABC group, Michel
Kemal, and with him we drove to one of the tourist boats
moored along the Nile and drank wine, and Adel gave me a
cheque for £100 on behalf of the Arabic Bureau for Cinema.
I gathered that it was some sort of 'token payment', to be used
for settling my bill at the Semiramis and for my expenses
generally, since I was the guest of the ABC. During the discussion on that boat it was decided to bring in a well-known film
producer called Zaki as 'production manager'—an idea which
was later dropped.

I wrote in my journal that night: 'I begin to wonder if the
ABC group are making this film because they care about
Palestine or because they hope to make some money?'

The following day we had another session with Fathi
Ibrahim, this time a lengthy one, during which he astonishingly
revealed that he wanted to bring in a producer from outside,
the Irish Brian Desmond Hurst, who had made some good
films, notably, *Tom Brown, Antony and Cleopatra,* and *The
Playboy of the Western World.* This was a shocker, and
Telmissany, when we told him, all but fainted dead away,
swearing that he would never, but never, ever, agree to it. In
fact they were all against it, and I was inclined to agree with
them that the film had to be an Arab production, though later,
when I met Brian Hurst in London, I came round to the idea
that there was everything to be said for having someone with

Western expertise on the job. The day after that Adel and I had the first of a series of sessions with the Jordanian ambassador, who was very nice, very co-operative—and very diplomatic.

We also went to the office of the Arab League—almost as impressive as the U.N. building in New York—to discuss the idea of reproducing my introduction to *The Road to Beersheba*, which is a concise statement of the historic facts as to how the Zionist state of 'Israel' came to be created, as a leaflet to be distributed in West Germany by the Arab Information office in Bonn. After which we met Abdel Khader to discuss the meeting with the Jordanian ambassador. That evening there arrived a telegram from Abu Zeid saying that he was 'in process of negotiating with the Egyptian authorities', which we none of us understood, for the Egyptian authorities were officially represented by the person of Fathi Ibrahim. We decided to leave it until we had seen the Jordanian ambassador again. . . .

I wrote in my journal that I longed to return to London, that I felt 'tired and depressed, and so tired of them all . . .'

Nevertheless next day I personally wired Abu Zeid that I had postponed my return to London for a few days in the hope of being present at the signing of the agreement between the Jordanian government and the Arabic Bureau for Cinema, 'the competent Egyptian authority'. But the agreement, I knew, would have to be approved by the Minister of Finance in Amman, and also by King Hussein. The sending of this telegram was an attempt to eliminate Ali Siam.

Whilst waiting for governmental developments we went on discussing the film in terms of the treatment of the scenario. Abdel Khader wanted to make it in two parts, the first part complete in itself; Adel objected that this would turn the film into a documentary, and the book must be filmed as a whole, and I supported him in this. The journal records: 'Adel got vehement to the point of anger, but when Arabs get angry like this it doesn't seem to matter; they say their piece and no ill-relations are established.'

There was the respite of a few days, and then a meeting of the ABC group at Adel's apartment, concerning which I wrote that 'it was quite as difficult as I had expected, in fact, known, it would be. Hassan and Michel and Abdel Khader will never agree to the film being done Adel's way, and Hassan was rude and aggressive. I suggested we should find a way out by having it done by an outsider—by Brian Hurst, for example, as proposed by Fathi Ibrahim—but no one wanted this. It had to be an *Arab* production. It was a complete impasse, and at about seven o'clock we ended the session, as Adel and I had to change for the dinner at the Jordanian ambassador's. . . .'

The following day Adel and I decided on drastic action. The Arabic Bureau for Cinema obviously could not continue in this state of dissension, and we taxied to some dingy offices to register some changes in the company's constitution; I didn't know then, and I don't know now, what they consisted of, but Adel was not a lawyer for nothing. None of it, anyhow, had any reality for me. It was just some complicated Egyptian bicker in which I had somehow become involved. I was resolved that when I had paid the Semiramis bill I would return the balance of the ABC money to Adel, and this I duly did. (I left it on his desk in his office, and he was so affronted that he would not even mention it.) It was resolved, on this day of decision, that Fathi Ibrahim's organisation should produce the film, with Brian Hurst, if he agreed, handling the first part, set in England, and Abdel Khader, if he agreed, handling the Jordanian part. What happened to Telmissany in all this I don't know, but according to my journal it meant that Hassan and Michel were out, and we went to the office of Adel's lawyer friend to draft a letter as from me to Adel cancelling my agreement with the ABC.

That was on November 11th. On the 17th I was, blessedly, back in London; but it was not the end of the story.

On 15 February, 1965, I took the typescript of my book about Jordan, *The Lovely Land,* to my publishers. I also read in *The Times* that King Hussein had reshuffled his cabinet and I noticed that Abu Zeid was no longer Minister of Information, or even in the cabinet. I wondered how this would affect the film project.

The next day I flew to Cairo, was duly met at the airport

by the faithful Adel, and checked in at the Semiramis—where a letter from Amman awaited me, urging me to contact the ambassador immediately and arrange to come as soon as possible to Amman. It was important I should meet the new Minister—whom I had met before and might remember . . .

In Cairo the now familiar pattern renewed itself; I had a great many people to see, articles to write, interviews to give, and there was endless discussion about the film—how to make it, who should make it. Two days after I got back Adel and I had an appointment with Fathi Ibrahim, and I recorded in my journal: 'Mr. Ibrahim very cordial and jolly, but somehow I got the feeling that he isn't all that serious about the film any more, though Adel doesn't agree. Astonishingly he said that he hadn't seen a copy of the book—given to him last November—and that he hadn't had a letter Adel had registered to him weeks ago. He is supposed to write to Dr. Hatim, asking him to write to the new Minister of Information in Amman, that COPRA (Fathi Ibrahim's organisation) represents the U.A.R. government in this film matter, so that he, Fathi Ibrahim, is the representative of Dr. Hatim for this purpose. But will he? I don't feel myself that he will. Or that the new Minister in Amman will be any more disposed to treat with anyone less than Dr. Hatim than was Adu Zeid.'

We were, it seemed to me, not merely back in square one, but bogged down there.

Meanwhile I received an official invitation from the new Minister in Amman to return there, the arrangements to be made through the ambassador in Cairo. I flew to Amman on the 24th, that is to say just a week after I arrived in Cairo. The day before I left I recorded in my journal: 'The situation regarding the film has changed, as it seems the Arab League is now to handle the matter. This resolves the differences between the Jordanian and the Egyptian governments, and cuts out, in all probability, both Fathi Ibrahim and Ali Siam. But I wonder what Adel's position will be in the rearrangements. He is convinced he will still be in on it, but I wonder. Yet for this purpose he is my lawyer, and he is the script writer.'

But curiouser and curiouser.

The day after I arrived in Amman I received at 8.40 a.m.

a request to present myself to the new Minister of Information
—who proved to be a cousin of the King, and a most charming
young man—at nine o'clock. Fortunately the Ministry is quite
close to the hotel and I arrived only a few minutes late. My
journal records: 'His Excellency had with him the Under
Secretary and the Chief of the Press Bureau, and a few minutes later there arrived Ali Siam, very spruce and shining and
smiling and self-assured and pleased with himself—as always.
It transpired that they had heard nothing in Amman about
the Arab League taking over the film, and they were as adamant as ever about it being made by a Western film company,
but nothing now will be decided until the meeting in Jerusalem
of Ministers of Information from the Arab States on April 19.
My own guess is that it will never be made. Ali Siam is still
talking about it being made with English actors, stars at that!
He will never give in. Nor will Adel. What happens if Ali really
does find a Western company to make it I can't imagine, for I
would then be in the impossible position of choosing between
the desire that the film should be made, for the sake of
Palestine, and personal loyalty to a friend. But the chances
seem more likely that it will never come to that.'

In the afternoon Ali arrived at the hotel with a mutual
friend, a Palestinian, from Jerusalem, and we had a long talk
about the film, but it was merely a repetition of the morning's
talk at the Ministry, and I recorded in my journal that I was
'so tired of it all.' When he left Ali said that he would be in
Jerusalem tomorrow, when I was, and I said, 'How frightful!'
He laughed and said I could never escape him, and reminded
me that in Kuwait in 1962 he had said that if ever I
wrote the Palestine novel I had said I might write he would
make a film of it. I remembered that he had said that, but I
hadn't taken it seriously at the time, for I had had then no
real idea for the novel, and I soon forgot both Ali Siam and
Kuwait. When he reminded me of it I felt only a weariness, and
just wished he would go away.

Which to all intents and purposes he did, for we did not
meet again; I had a heavy programme arranged for me in
Jordan, and after an exhausting nine days I flew back to Cairo
—where with Adel I went within a day or two of my return

to the Arab League to discuss the film. I recorded in my journal that I felt tired and depressed, and 'I don't believe in the Arab League in connection with the film. It will probably be years before they start anything, and in the meantime the talk will go on—in the League, and in Amman, but the Jordanians are more serious, I begin to think, even though wrong-headed.'

It seems odd, now, in retrospect, that I thought the Jordanians wrong-headed—by which I meant in their insistence that the film should be made by a Western company—for obviously if it was to be made it should be made as expertly as possible, and English actors would be needed for at least the first part of the story.

Within a week I was back in London—only to return to Cairo a fortnight later as delegate to the Palestine Students' Conference. This was an experience I tremendously enjoyed, and not least because my old friend, and friend of Reginald's, from the thirties, Nevill Barbour, the distinguished Arabist, was in the party of British delegates. We were put up in one of the smaller new hotels, the Nile, which faced across the river to the University at which the Conference was held. At the opening session the huge auditorium was packed with some eight thousand students, chanting slogans, reciting Arabic poetry, and liberating Palestine in the endless torrent of Arabic oratory . . . But that is another story, and it here remains to conclude the story of that perishing film project, and perish it did, from the moment it was handed over to the Arab League.

At the end of the Conference, which lasted about nine days, the delegates were flown to Jerusalem, and when our programme was completed there, and in Amman, and Jericho—where we were entertained by the P.L.O. in a hotel on the shores of the Dead Sea—I did not fly back with the others to London but stayed on for the wedding of a Palestinian friend. Two days after that I returned to Cairo, and it was by then Easter.

Cairo seemed stuffy and dusty after Jordan, with its deep green valleys and wonderful broad-screen vistas, and I wrote in my journal that I was 'still in Jerusalem, with its strange, heart-breaking beauty, and the lean, dark faces of the Palestinians.' I stayed again in the Nile hotel, where I had an

eighth floor room with a fine view out over the river to the
desert and the Pyramids, and as always in Cairo I met a great
many people and did a great many things, and some of it was
interesting, and much of it was fatiguing, and there was no
real point in any of it. My relationship with Adel had somehow
deteriorated; he was moody and irritable, and we were inclined
to bicker. It was, in fact, all over—the film project, the friendship, and, in a sense, Cairo itself. I was glad to leave, inside a
week, and at the airport felt dead inside, and there was nothing
left to say. I felt that I would never want to return to Cairo—
that there would be no point in doing so—and I never have.
But that I would always want to return to Jordan—and three
months later, in July, I did return, invited once more again as
an official guest.

The object of the return this time was to get background
material for another Palestine novel* I planned, designed to
speak for the Resistance, already in 1965 a growing force, as
The Road to Beersheba had spoken for the 1948 refugees from
Lydda. There was a young Palestinian I had met in the huge
Ein es Sultan refugee camp in Jericho I needed to talk with, to
visit in his home there; and high on the agenda was the official
meeting with King Hussein, about which I was not enthusiastic,
for I had already met him several times unofficially, and the
official visit was by then too late for the Jordan book. But since
it was required of me to have this official interview I was resolved to use it as a final effort to try and find out what was
happening about The Film.

The King was not in Amman when I arrived and did not
return from Paris until two days later, and I was then taken to
the airport as a member of the official reception. I recorded
in my journal that there were flags and big crowds, and that we
waited on a terrace with a number of village notables in very
white head-dresses and gallibiehs, and a number of Army
officers, and ministers. 'Below, we saw the Prime Minister, and
the British ambassador. Ali Siam was much in evidence, taking
"movie" pictures. We had a brief friendly conversation.' But
there was no mention of the film. It was not our last encounter,
for we were to meet again in London in the near future, but

* *The Night and its Homing*, 1966.

our paths did not cross again that last time in Jordan, and we did not seek each other out. All of us who had been on the terrace were duly received by the King, but it was another twelve days before I was summoned to the Palace for the official interview. We were alone, as I had been with Nasser, but I do not find it as easy to talk to a man seated behind his desk in an office as in his own home, but I did tell His Majesty about the new Palestine novel, and I did ask him about the film. 'Is it lost forever in the *oubliettes* of the Arab League in Cairo?' I asked. He smiled and did not offer an opinion, but made a note on a pad on his desk and said he would inquire about it, and we then talked of other things.

Whether he ever did inquire about the film I have no idea, and the next time we met was in London, in his suite at the Grosvenor Hotel, in November, 1967, six months after the June war, and we had much more then on our hearts and minds than the film that never was and now never would be.

3

A mansaf *with the Beersheba* bedu

When I was in Amman the first time in the series of 1965 visits
I received a telegram of greetings 'from the Beersheba bedouin
tribes'; the sender was Izzat Atawneh of Hebron—a well-
known personality, I learned, and sheikh of twenty-seven
tribes. In 1948, when Beersheba became part of 'Israel', the
bedu fled into the deserts around Hebron. This small Muslim
town was then, of course, and until 1967, part of Jordan. It
was arranged, by those in charge of my programme, that I
should meet Atawneh when I was next in Jerusalem, and this
I duly did, in the office of Anton Albina, a Christian Palestinian. I found the effusiveness of his homage to the great and
noble author of *The Road to Beersheba* 'a bit much,' as I
recorded in my journal, but by the time we had eaten shish-
kebab together, with Anton Albina, and Tahir Shihabi, the-
man-from-the-Information-Office who was looking after me in
Jerusalem, I got used to him and when we parted had accepted
his invitation to visit Hebron as his guest. I fully intended to
do this, but I had a heavy programme in Jordan at that time
and had to get back to Cairo, and it didn't work out. It was
not until I was in Jerusalem six months later, in August, that
I fulfilled my promise to Izzat Atawneh—who had by then
become Abu Sultan, 'the father of Sultan,' his son having
distinguished himself at the university, thereby having confer-
red honour on his father who, in the Arab fashion, was hence-
forth proud to be known as *Abu*, 'the father of . . .'

I had been in Hebron in 1962, very briefly, on my first visit to Bethlehem, the road to which, from Jerusalem, continues on, and had liked the feeling of height in Hebron—it is higher than Jerusalem—and its antiquity, but had found its intensely Muslim atmosphere somewhat oppressive. It was a pervasive Muslim puritanism which excluded even a cinema— about which the young men complained bitterly, and those that could escaped to Jerusalem and Amman. That first time I had been taken to the mosque—originally a Crusader church— and was in some trouble because I wore a dress the sleeves of which finished above the elbow, so that the keeper of the mosque had to find a little shawl with which to cover my nakedness. (Fortunately he hadn't noticed that I had bare legs.) During that visit I was also taken to the furnace where oddments of thrown-away glass, mostly Coca-Cola bottles, are melted down to be refashioned into the beautiful blue Hebron glassware.

On this second visit to Hebron the Palestinian friend of my Jericho days of 1962, Sufian Alami, who had first shown me something of the town, was again with me, and a kinsman, Abdel Karim Alami, of Ramallah, who was to be killed at the Allenby Bridge, alas and alas, in June, 1967. We drove from Jerusalem, with Tahir Shihabi, through fertile lands green with vineyards, and outside the police barracks in Hebron our host, Izzat Atawneh, Abu Sultan, sheikh of the Beersheba tribes, awaited us in full bedouin regalia, gleaming white robes and head-dress, and, as I recorded in my journal, 'revolver, knife, and all!'

We drove, inevitably, to the mosque, and this time I needed no little shawl. I admired some handsome stained glass windows, and gazed respectfully at the reputed tombs of Abraham and Leah, covered with green brocade. Though what impressed me more was an outside kitchen where a sheep was being cooked whole in a vast cauldron, with maize, or corn of some kind, for distributing to the local poor, or, I was told, anyone who wished to taste 'holy food'. For this pious cause people donate sheep, and it was a regular Friday event. Small thin children waited with tin containers for hunks of fat meat. Gaunt cats also waited. But we continued on our way without tasting holy food, for not a sheep but lambs were already being cooked at the house of Abu Sultan.

Before proceeding to the house we visited the Tree of Abraham, an incredibly ancient ilex tree with a shell of a trunk, enclosed by railings—an oak tree, I was assured (and in California, I was to discover, they call these ilex trees oaks— 'live oaks') and veritably the tree under which Abraham received the news from three heavenly visitors, as he sat at his tent door, in the heat of the day, in the plains of Mamre, that old and well stricken in years as he and his wife Sarah were— she was ninety, and he was nearly a hundred—they should produce a son, and Sarah laughed, but it was so, as is set forth in the book of Genesis. Certainly this tree could be a thousand years old, but as old as Abraham? *Ma'alesh,* as the Arabs say, 'never mind.' For those interested in such details, the 'oak of Mamre', as it is called, is 'maintained' by the Russian Orthodox Church, which has—or anyhow had—a convent nearby.

Abu Sultan's house was approached by a long path under an arbour of vines, then, in August, heavy with luscious green grapes. The path ended in a wide terrace, also hung with vines, where it would have been pleasant to have sat, I felt, but formality required that we should repair to a long reception room, with chairs and settees ranged along the walls. Here we were served cold lemon drinks, very welcome in the heat, it being by then around noon. A steady procession of notabilities arrived, and at one point Abu Sultan ran out and fired his revolver into the air in celebration. The guests included His Eminence the mayor—he is an Eminence because he is a religious sheikh, not merely tribal—wearing flowing robes and the high red pill-box turban denoting his religious office. His Excellency the Governor came, and many bedouin sheikhs, refugees from Beersheba. A member of the distinguished Al-Husseini family of Jerusalem was also there; this Husseini had spent years in prison during the British Mandate, when the Palestinians were struggling for independence, in the thirties, and in 1950 was charged with Musa Husseini—who had been to Oak Cottage, and whom Reginald and I had liked very much, a very charming young man—and three others with the assassination of King Abdullah. Musa and the others were hanged, but this Husseini was discharged. He told me, on that Hebron occasion, that he had witnessed the hangings, which he described to me, and I could wish that he hadn't. . . .

The room filled up and overflowed on to the terrace, and finally, when all the guests had arrived, I was asked, as the guest for whom the occasion had been arranged, to lead the way to where the great feast, the *mansaf*, had been spread out on long tables in an adjoining room. I do not remember, now, how many lambs, cooked whole, were curled up, complete with their heads, on great mounds of rice, but there were several. There is no cutlery on these occasions; hands are washed at an outside tap before approaching the festive board, and then pieces of meat are torn from the steaming carcases and hands delve deep into the mounds of rice . . . over which hot greasy water, in which the meat has been boiled, is constantly poured by diligently attending servants. Abu Sultan continually tore off hunks of the meet to hand to me, commanding me, exultantly, to Eat! Eat! It was just too bad that I have never been a great meat eater, and that fat and grease are for me very great evils, my digestion and liver appalled by them, but I did my best, God help me, I did my best, laughing off, as best I could, my host's protests that I had the appetite of a bird.

It was a relief when, after handwashing at the tap in the yard, again, a servant in attendance with soap and towels, we all adjourned to consume cold hunks of melon—red watermelon, white melon, yellow melon—and take short sips of the bitter bedouin coffee served black and scalding hot from huge brass beakers.

After all this an inspector of education made a long speech in Arabic, translated to me, word for word, by Sufian Alami, at my side. It was in praise of the guest of honour as a defender of the Palestinian cause. I replied to this in English, my speech translated, sentence by sentence, into Arabic by Sufian. Finally Abu Sultan read a terrific tribute in English to our Great Good Friend, 'who stands with the Palestinian Arabs, and with the Arabs from the ocean to the Gulf,' with a reference to 'your glorious book, *The Road to Beersheba*, and your marvellous poem, *Falastine Arabiyeh*,' and to whom, the citation continued, 'the hearts and doors of Arabs everywhere are open.'

At the conclusion of this I was presented with an Arab head-dress, which Abu Sultan insisted on placing on my head, though I protested that it was a man's head-dress, but they all laughed and clapped and were happy, and the nonsense was soon terminated by the arrival of Land Rovers from the Army to take us to the road to Beersheba, at the border, south of Hebron. I was in the leading vehicle, with a captain who was a Circassian, and who, with his blue eyes and fair hair and moustache, could have been English. I did not at all want to do this trip to the border again; I had done it with Sufian Alami, from Jericho, in 1962, when I was writing *The Road to Beersheba*, and it had been a poignant experience which I did not care to repeat. I had gone then, by permission of the Military, some distance along the road to Beersheba, which was—and still is—in 'Israel'. It is very rough-going after leaving the border village of Dhahiriya, which I described in the novel, and it was all as I had remembered it, and then, all over again, I stood looking across the deep valley to the hillside *kibbutz* in Occupied Territory, and, as Abdel Karim Alami put it, 'the scene of Anton Mansour's tragic death'. . . .

We walked a little over some rough ground so that Abu Sultan could point out his brother's house in Occupied Territory; they had not been able to see or correspond with each other for seventeen years; he did not even know if his brother was still alive and living in that house. . . . All over again there was the upsurge of grief and bitterness and anger. In the distance the town of Beersheba was visible, but the ground on which we stood was Beersheba district, and dotted about in the stony wilderness were the black tents of the Beersheba bedouins, the refugee *bedu* of the Beersheba tribes.

Then back to Dhahiriya, to the military H.Q., for a wash-and-brush-up. A young officer handed me a towel and waited whilst I washed, then took the towel from me, raised it to his lips, then reverently folded and smoothed it. 'This I will keep always, as a souvenir of the author of *The Road to Beersheba*,' he solemnly declared.

F

We then piled back into the Land Rovers and drove to a long black tent at the side of a dusty road, the desert flowing away behind. A white flag had been hoisted above the tent— denoting the presence of an honoured guest, Abu Sultan explained. The tent was open its entire length facing the road. At one end carpets and cushions had been arranged; on the uncarpeted two-thirds of the tent a number of tribesmen sat on the ground. When we entered they all rose to their feet and I was presented to each one; there was no handshaking, but to each one I gave the Arabic salutation, *Marhaba.* Then we all disposed ourselves on the carpets and cushions and thin mattresses spread on the ground, Abu Sultan, Sufian, Abdel Karim, the Governor, Tahir Shihabi, the Circassian captain, and myself, leaning with our right arms on the piled-up cushions; we were joined by the sheikh of the tribe, and the paramount sheikh—sheikh of all the Beersheba *bedu*—and after the rhythmic, musical pounding of the beans, with pestles in wooden tubs, coffee was served from brass beakers into tiny handleless cups, to be swallowed in a single sip and the cup handed back for refilling, or turned down to denote no more.

There followed the inevitable complimentary speeches in praise of the guest of honour, then, to my dismay, a *mansaf* was set before us—another sheep cooked whole and set upon a giant mound of rice. We had had the lengthy repast at Hebron at two o'clock, and it was by then only six, and after the first *mansaf* I had felt that I would never eat again. How to cope again, and so soon? But Abu Sultan let me off lightly this time, merely scooping some of the brains out of the sheep's head for me, though he and the others ate as heartily as though it was the first meal of their day. I felt very badly about it, with the gaunt tribesmen at the far side of the tent looking on, for I knew that these bedouins were desperately poor, being refugees, the Israelis having confiscated their lands, and that as they were not in camps they received only half-rations from U.N.W.R.A.—and the full rations were meagre to the point of bare subsistence level, so that supplementary rations had to be issued to the children, who suffered from malnutrition. How could these people afford to kill one of their sheep for this *mansaf*? I asked. But everyone seemed to think it was all right,

and Abu Sultan went so far as to declare that it was right
and proper; some sacrifice it was right to make for their great
friend, the author of *The Road to Beersheba*, the great book
which defended their cause. 'You make sacrifices for us!' he
asserted. Did I? I wondered. Sometimes in the hot Jerusalem
nights I thought I did, itching all over with mosquito and
sand-fly bites, and by day feeling sick from the heat, and exhausted from giving-out so continuously to so many people,
and being bumped in Land Rovers over rough terrain without being consulted as to what I would like to do . . . sometimes
I thought I did. I wrote in my journal, apropos: 'But they
consider that I belong to them, and people do what they like
with what belongs to them. Which is why they continually
make new translations of *Beersheba*—the latest is running as a
serial, in Arabic, in a Saudi Arabia newspaper—and there are
new radio versions, and now, it seems, it is being dramatised as
a stage-play. They *tell* me; it never occurs to them to *ask* me; it
is theirs . . . And "all Arabs like you," they tell me. Endlessly
and everywhere they tell me. And thank me; endlessly they
thank me. And I could weep because I feel I do so little, not
from lack of willing, but from sheer inability. And now they
have the poem I wrote for them, *Falastine Arabiyeh*, "Palestine
is Arab", and this, too, will be endlessly translated—has already
been—and will circulate from the Mediterranean to the Gulf.
It has already been done in Syria, Lebanon, and Jordan, and
the P.L.O. are distributing it as a leaflet, here, in English, with
decorations by Ismael Shammout, the Palestinian artist, and
my short piece on Jerusalem, *The Divided City,* is part of the
leaflet, and of all this I am glad, but it is so terribly little, and
the gratitude disproportionate. . . .'

Well, but anyway we dealt with the *mansaf,* and then the
old paramount sheikh expressed a wish that I should meet his
three wives 'and many children', so we crossed the road to a
stone-built hut in which the harem was gathered for this occasion, and as we approached the women set up those shrill
ululations traditional for special occasions. I had heard them
in Morocco, in the autumn of 1951, when the crowds lined
the streets of Rabat on Friday when the Sultan (there was no
'King' then) passed to the mosque; and I had heard them in

Jordan in October last year, when I had been in the convoy with King Hussein on his tour of the North—the salutation of the women. Now I was to hear these ululations—*ululululu-uuu*—in honour of myself.

Inside the hut the women shook hands, eagerly, with strong grips, and I spoke to them through Sufian. Some of them were beautiful and most of them good-looking, and the young ones all had babies in their arms or toddlers clutching their long skirts. I never sorted out which were the wives of the sheikh— and there were so many of them. They lived with their husbands and families in the black goat hair tents scattered all over the sandy hillsides of the Beersheba district, at the border, beyond the village of Dhahiriya.

The paramount sheikh told me, through Sufian, that I must come again and spend two nights in their tents, and they would do the *bedu* dances for me. . . .

I would have been interested in the dancing, but I knew that I could not have borne the discomfort, nor the eating of their food, of which they have so little. I therefore smiled and murmured *Insh' Allah*, which the sheikh repeated. *Insh' Allah* —God willing. That most useful of phrases, serving so many occasions.

All this over we drove to the outskirts of Hebron, where the local ladies were gathered to meet me, giving an enormous tea party, though it was by then late in the evening, and I was also, by then, exhausted. But one by one the ladies were presented to me, and little speeches were made, and I drank their tea, and nibbled at least one of their cakes, and smiled and smiled until my face ached with it.

It was over at last. Everything is over at last, and Sufian and Abdel Karim and Tahir Shihabi and I were in Sufian's car driving back to Jerusalem, but it was not an end of the gaieties, for as we drove along a stretch of road where the Israelis were only a few yards away on the sides of the low hills a shot rang out. There were no other cars on the road at that time, which meant they were potting at us. The Israeli guards took potshots at passing cars, it seemed, and when they had 'winged' enough the news reached Hebron and the road was closed—which was apparently a source of Israeli satisfaction.

Sufian drew the car in under a wall and switched off the lights. Whilst we were debating what to do the lights of an oncoming car loomed up and we decided to go on—under its cover, the oncoming car providing a new target for the snipers.

We got back to Jerusalem without further incident, all of us dropping with tiredness. It had been a very long day.

4

Incident by the Barada river, Damascus

In November, 1966, I was invited to Damascus as the guest of the Syrian newspaper, *Al Thawra.* I had not been in Syria since 1962 and was delighted to accept. At that time I believed the Syrian Arab Republic to be the most militant of the Arab countries vis-à-vis 'Israel' and the liberation of Palestine. Also, although I was not drawn to the Ba'ath, the 'Renaissance' party, it would be interesting to see what it was achieving in Syria. I flew to Damascus on the 17th and was back in London on the 28th, after an exhausting ten days—an official visit reckons to be ten days—during which I met the Head of State (there was officially no 'President'), the Prime Minister, various other ministers, trade union leaders, the chief of the National Guard, the leader of a peasants' organisation, Governors, Army chiefs, leaders of women's organisations, members of Al Asifa, the military wing of Al Fatah—and a great many journalists. My activities were reported daily in the press, accompanied by hideous photographs, and I was trailed everywhere by television cameras. I mention all this not in any spirit of self-aggrandisement but to indicate that I had a very full programme during those ten days and to explain the morning by the Barada river, the result of a plea, half way, for a morning off—just a few hours, I begged, in which to be alone, free of cameramen with lights, and journalists asking what I had come to think of as the Usual Questions—to which it was only possible to give what I had also come to think of as the Usual Answers. . . .

My request seemed reasonable, and I was given a morning off. I should be back at the hotel by two o'clock for the drive to the restaurant on the Beirut road for the *Al Thawra* luncheon, but until then I was free.

The free morning, however, did not quite work out, for I stayed in the hotel after breakfast to write a few letters, and was overtaken by the arrival of three students who wished to discuss with me well, what else, The Palestine Situation. They were nice young people and the discussion took some time, and it might have gone on much longer but that a man from *Al Marifa* magazine came to pay me for an article I had written for them in London at the instigation of the Syrian Chargé d'Affaires. This also involved conversation, and it was around one before I got out for the walk I had promised myself after five days of being whisked from place to place by car. I should have gone out immediately after breakfast, of course, but, still, I had an hour, and I would just stroll along the little tree-lined Barada river, only part of which had been covered over, despite the threat in 1962 that it was all to be sacrificed to make a car park.

So I set out, shaking my head at the importuning shoe-shine boys, regarding the old balconied houses with pleasure, looking across the little river to the wall-enclosed Old City, and the house from which St. Paul is supposed to have escaped from an upper window, and the Street called Strait, and wishing I had set out earlier, with time to explore all that, but I strolled along, enjoying the warm bright morning, happy to be walking instead of driving, enjoying the brief interlude of freedom. At a small bridge across the river I paused, debating with myself whether I would cross and walk back along the other side, resting a little, and looking—just looking; savouring.

Whilst I stood there, idly, a good-looking boy I would have thought not more than about sixteen, or even less, approached and stood beside me. 'The Barada river, Madame,' he said, in only slightly accented English.

'I know,' I said, smiling, adding that I was glad it had not all been covered in. He regarded me intently, then said, 'You have been in there, Madame?', indicating the *Exposition* ground behind us.

'No,' I said, 'there's nothing on in there just now.'

He said, with a curious urgency, 'But you can go in. It is very nice in there. Come with me, Madame. I will show you. We can go for a walk. We can sit on the grass,' and he repeated, urgently, 'It is very nice in there!'

I said, hardly less urgently, acutely embarrassed, 'I have to get back to the hotel. *Ma'as salama!*' and turned away, towards the bridge.

He came close, then, holding out a bare, golden-brown arm.

'Look, Madame! We are the same colour!' He was fair-skinned, with brown hair; he could have been Circassian.

I moved resolutely towards the bridge, quite desperate to get away . . . to escape an absurd, impossible, situation.

'*Ma'as salama,*' I repeated. The Arabic farewell—goodbye, God go with you. Said curtly it can be dismissive. I said it curtly. It was all preposterous—tiresome; I wanted out. . . .

He blocked my way to the bridge—young, lithe, so good-looking, and so curiously desperate.

'I love you, Madame!' he astonishingly said, and repeated in a crescendo of vehemence, 'I love you, I love you, I love you!'

I pushed past him, then, towards a group of white-robed Arabs gossiping at the corner of the bridge; they looked up, mildly curious—a Western woman, walking alone; but not a young woman, so of no great interest.

At the other side of the bridge I looked back. The youth, haversack slung over a shoulder, was strolling towards the *Exposition* grounds. He did not turn his head. Whatever he had wanted of the Western woman it had not worked out. He went on his way.

And I went on mine, profoundly puzzled, and somewhat annoyed that my stroll along the river had been spoiled. What on earth did it mean? I asked myself; and I still wonder. Could so attractive a youth have been so sexually deprived that even a woman old enough to be his grandmother would do? Even if I looked ten years younger than the sixty-six I then was—and I do not think I did—I would still be, by Middle East standards, *old*. Sex outside of marriage is difficult to come by in

Muslim cities, but Damascus has many Christians, and Christians are notoriously lax in their morals, and there would have been accommodating Christian girls available to the young man, one would have thought. Could it be that he didn't know the meaning of the words he uttered with such urgency? Yet their very urgency suggested that he did. And that business of stretching out his bare arm beside mine and saying that we had the same coloured skins—why that? To dispose of any colour prejudice the Western woman might have? But like many Arabs he was light-skinned, and fairer than some.

Perhaps it was a simple pickpocket ruse to get me into the *Exposition* grounds, and then— But the grounds were not deserted; people went in there freely, when, as then, they were not in use. And in my jersey suit I hadn't, really, any pockets to pick, and wore no jewellery. Nor would I have been carrying a handbag for a short stroll along the river.

A young friend of mine who knows the Middle East suggests that it was simply that I was a woman walking alone and could therefore be presumed to be 'fair game' for a hunting male. I protested that I had walked alone and unmolested in the shopping thoroughfares of Damascus, as in other Arab towns and cities. 'Ah, but you were not in a shopping thoroughfare,' my friend pointed out, 'you were wandering outside the town, some distance out; also you were *loitering* at the bridge. . . .'

'Not with intent,' I protested.

'The young man wasn't to know that. So far as he was concerned you were worth a try.'

'At my age?'

'Age doesn't necessarily come into it.'

Perhaps; I don't know. I cannot say that anyone's guess is as good as mine for I have no guess.

In retrospect I half wish I had seen the adventure through and gone with him into the grounds. Perhaps we should have done no more than sit on the grass whilst he practised his English on me? Or perhaps it really was a sex thing and he knew of some secluded place in those grounds?

I shall never know, and I do but report the strange tale of a morning stroll beside the Barada river.

5

The Children's Things

To the extent that I am telling this story as though it were recounted to me personally by the Palestinian friend whose tragedy it was, when in fact we did not have that conversation and I was told it in a letter, this is a fictionised version; but the facts are true. The alternative to telling it like this is merely to set forth the letter, and it is necessary to fill in the background.

I received this letter from Amman in the winter of 1967; my friend was there as a refugee from Hebron, which was occupied by the Israelis in the June war. He was then, like so many Palestinians, a refugee for the second time; as a boy of twelve he had been, with his family, a refugee from his native Lydda, from which, and the surrounding area, a hundred thousand people had been expelled by the Israelis in July, 1948, at a moment's notice, mostly women and children and old men, the young men having all been rounded-up. 'Glubb Pasha,' Lieutenant-General Sir John Bagot Glubb, has an account of this in his book, *A Soldier with the Arabs*,* and says in it, 'We shall never know how many children died'. But he omits to mention what my Palestinian friend, and other Palestinians who were in that terrible enforced exodus, told me, which is that the people were not allowed to travel along the roads but were driven into the burning wilderness—the temperature was a hundred degrees in the shade—on a trek to Ramallah, in

* 1957.

Jordan, which became a massacre, with the old and the young dying of sunstroke and thirst, and such things happening as I could not bring myself to describe in the novel I wrote based on it, *The Road to Beersheba*,* written as a 'reply' to Leon Uri's *Exodus*—as part of the story of the *other* exodus—the enforced exodus of a million Palestinian Arabs from their homes and lands.

Khalil—I will call him that—was my first close Palestinian friend. We first met in Jordan in 1962, and there developed a friendship and affection which has endured to this day, though we have not met since I was last in Amman in 1965. He went to Hebron in 1966 and was there overtaken by the June war in '67. He is now in Kuwait.

We had many such urgent, intense conversations in the lounge of that hotel in Amman, though not this one; but in telling it like this something of his personality is perhaps conveyed, as well as the background.

When I entered the Intercontinental hotel Khalil was waiting for me. The vast lounge was almost empty; three or four men sat at the far side, round a low table, in earnest discussion—U.N. observers, I thought, or British M.P.s out for a quick run-around. Tourists had been thin on the ground since the June war. Khalil strode across the wide open space of the tiled floor to meet me. He was as I had remembered him from three years ago, in 1965, darkly handsome, with a warm smile, and still only in his thirties. He was the same, yet there was something different; there were lines at each side of his mouth now and his charming smile seemed not to reach his eyes.

As he took my hand he was all apologies for not bringing me to his brother's house, explaining that it was full of relatives, and so many children—everyone had come there from Jerusalem and Ramallah and all over. We couldn't talk there; I would understand.

I said that of course I understood, and why didn't we go and sit outside on the verandah, where it would be cooler. We went outside and a thin, sad-looking young man brought us cold drinks. He was from one of the refugee camps just outside

* 1963.

Amman—the whole staff were, and had been since long before the June war.

When we were settled Khalil leaned forward, eagerly.

'I had to talk to you,' he said. 'I have to tell someone. Someone from outside. Someone sympathetic—an old friend, from the old days.' He paused a moment, brooding, then went on, 'I have always been able to talk to you. When I was engaged to Selma—all the family complications—the money arrangements. All those talks we had in Jerusalem, and here in Amman. I should have stayed here—then none of it would have happened. I had a good job here, and Selma had friends. We should never have gone to Hebron.'

The bitterness in his voice was intense.

I said, 'You were offered a better job in Hebron—it was natural to accept. You wanted the best for yourself and Selma and the children. You had a nice house there—far better than you had here. You never liked it here, and you couldn't forsee what would happen.'

He assented, eagerly. 'That was it. That was the biggest part of it. Ever since we were turned out of Lydda in 1948 I'd wanted to be back on the West Bank—to feel myself in *Palestine* again! If it had been only the money I could have gone to Kuwait—I had the opportunity. But Hebron offered the chance to live and work in Palestine, and I made the decision. We had a nice home and it was healthy for the children—not hot and dusty in the summer as it is in Amman. We had a fine place there. You know—you saw it.'

'Yes,' I confirmed. 'It was a nice place.'

'Then that terrible morning in June last year, when we knew it was all over and all we could think of was to get out. There were people who stayed. We had neighbours who did—they hadn't had our 1948 experience. Those of us who knew what it could be like panicked. Those of us who had cars piled our families into them. I had ten people in my car. I had to get to Jerusalem, where my mother and sister were. When we got there they had already left to go to my brother in Amman. My mother panicked, remembering Lydda . . .'

All this I knew, but I also knew that he had to tell me again. He had never told it in person before; only written it. Now he could fill in the details, speak out of his heart, and he had the compulsion to do so.

'We were fortunate in having my brother to go to,' he went on. 'Poor Adnan, all but crowded out of his house! And in trouble himself, too, with his business in Jerusalem lost to him, taken over by the Israelis. We didn't pack anything that morning we left Hebron. We grabbed the children and piled into the car, and people piled in with us. I suppose that as in 1948 we believed that somehow we'd be back before long. Until it happened I think we never really believed the Israelis would move in and occupy us, town by town, village by village. But they moved in, and then no one could move out, and the months went by and we had only the clothes we had run out in and what we could get from friends and relatives, and in the hot summer that was all right, but then summer was over and it began to get cold in Amman and we thought of the good warm clothes we had left in Hebron, and the children really needed them. Selma kept repeating why didn't I apply for a permit to go to Hebron and fetch the children's things. They couldn't refuse us *that*. I said that people who could napalm refugees on the roads could refuse anything. But Selma said *that* was war. The war was over now and they had won and everything had quietened down, and the military were in our house, some Israeli officers, and what good were the children's things to them? I should apply for permission to go. Friends who had stayed on in Hebron might be able to put in a word for us. And so on, and so on. I didn't believe in the plan, but Selma kept on and on about it, and when the baby got bronchitis she cried and said it was because the poor little thing had no warm clothing, and there were all those good woollen things in our house, and what use were they to the Israeli officers? The children's things . . .

'My mother agreed with Selma. She said I should try and go, and Adnan's wife also said so. She had no more clothes to give or lend, she said; no one had, any more; there were too many of us in need. She was beginning to be out of sympathy with us because there were too many of us crowded into the house, living on top of each other, and she and Adnan had their own children, their own problems.

'So with Adnan's help I put in an application. The Israelis were letting people in at that time, and it wasn't so difficult. I got the permit and Selma gave me a list of the things she wanted, with notes about where to find them. Of course, if I could get any of our own things, winter overcoats and pullovers and such, and her red woollen dress and tweed skirt, so much the better. I'd thought, too, I might be able to collect a few of my books. I hadn't wanted to make this trip, but once I had the permit I became excited, and hopeful.

'It was a strange experience going back, with all the checkposts, ours as well as theirs, and soldiers everywhere. It took so long even to reach Jerusalem, though I took the new road through Jericho—not going through the town; I specially didn't want to go through the town; it had too many memories. Going down to Jericho, and up to Jerusalem—those were the good days! But there was no way of by-passing Jerusalem. It was terrible to be in Jerusalem—occupied Jerusalem. You can't imagine.'

He stubbed out his cigarette and lit another, his hands not quite steady.

'I can imagine,' I said, quietly. 'I, also, loved Jerusalem. *Arab* Jerusalem. It's better not to talk about it. You got through Jerusalem and out on to the Hebron road . . .'

'Yes. So close to the border. The Israelis used to snipe at the passing cars, at the tyres, just to remind us they were still there. They don't have to do that now. They're everywhere now—a locust swarm. I got back to Hebron and there was a soldier on guard at the gate to my house—the gate that leads into the vine arbour, if you remember, up to the front door. I showed the soldier my permit and he let me through. At the front door there was another soldier, and I explained to him that it had been my house and that I had come in the hope of being allowed to collect a few clothes for my children. I spoke in Arabic and he replied in Arabic that my permit did not say I could call at the house but only that I could be in Hebron, and that I should not have been let through. I think he was an Iraqi, from the way he spoke, an Iraqi Jew, and I addressed him as a brother Arab and pleaded with him to fetch someone to speak with me about my request, but this made him angry and he said he was not my brother but an Israeli soldier, and he would not take my message for I had no right to be there and should clear out at once. Then I became angry and shouted at him that, no, he was not my brother Arab and wherever he was born in the Arab world he had no Arab heart, and I tried to push past him and through the French windows at the front door of my house, and he fired his rifle into the air and other soldiers came running, and they rushed at me, and grabbed me, and I kept shouting that I wanted to see an officer, and I struggled and hit out, and in the middle of all this confusion an officer came and the soldiers fell back, and the soldier looked at me and asked what I wanted. He spoke in English, with a strong accent. I think perhaps he was German. I told him, "This was my house, and I ask permission to enter and collect my children's clothes. We are living in Amman now, and it is cold there in winter." He asked to see my permit, and I showed it to him; he looked at it and handed it back. He said, "Your house has been requisitioned by the Israeli Army. It is not permitted to remove anything from requisitioned property." I told him, "I don't ask for anything except the children's winter clothes. They are in the bottom drawer of the chest in the big bedroom." He said again, "It is not allowed to remove anything from requisitioned property," then motioned to a soldier and said, "Take him away."

'The soldier grabbed my arm, but I jerked myself free and faced the officer again. "The *children's things*," I said. "I only want the *children's things!*" He turned and walked away, and two soldiers seized me and marched me out of the house and down the path under the vine arbour, and all the time I was struggling and crying out, "The children's things! Just the children's things!" When they reached the gate where the guard stood they shoved me through it, violently, and I fell on my face into the dust of the road.'

He looked at me.

'Do you understand it?' he asked, then repeated, helplessly, 'I only wanted the *children's things...*'

I said nothing. For a few minutes we sat in silence, then I said, at last, heavily, 'Perhaps before I leave we could go shopping together and you and Selma will allow me to buy some warm clothing for the children.'

His eyes filled with tears.

'You are very kind. But I have to tell you—there is only one child now. The little one—developed pneumonia. She died. Yes. It probably would have made no difference if the Israeli officer had said yes. But Selma will never believe it. Well, there it is. Now with the other child we are going to Kuwait. This is why I had to see you—to say goodbye . . .'

PART III

Greek Steamer to Alex, 1964

I

Venice Revisited

In the spring of 1964 I arranged to travel to Cairo by Greek ship from Venice to Alexandria, and thence by train, being tired of flying. The object of the journey was to attend a conference in Cairo convened by the General Union of Palestine Students there. On the morning of my departure I received a letter from Gaza telling me that the conference had been postponed until July. This was all the more exasperating as the Palestininan friend who wrote to me knew that I would be travelling by ship and had arrangements to make, and I had asked him to cable me confirming the date. I had been expecting a cable all the week, from either Gaza or Cairo, and had been puzzled by its non-arrival. I had been resolved not to re-visit Cairo at that time except to attend the conference, and had let this be known. Had I been flying I would have cancelled the trip when I received that letter, but I had booked a passage in a Greek ship that was sailing next day and cancellation did not seem feasible. I was very put out, but decided to go ahead, telling myself that there were things I could usefully do in Cairo, and that I had anyhow always wanted to see Athens and Rhodes, and I was sure to enjoy revisiting Venice, where I had not been since the twenties, and I had Greek-Egyptian friends in Alex....

I recovered from my irritation on the train journey to Dover, telling myself, philosophically, that the Arabs were after all the Irish of the East, all warmth and charm and unreliability, and a Middle East Old Hand had told me, years ago, that if you loved them it was no use complaining; you just had to accept them.

The English Channel was flat and grey, and it was nice to see it again, and the cliffs of Dover were misty, and it was nice to see them, too; but once aboard I saw no more of the sea, repairing immediately to the bar, as is my custom on such journeys.

But the four-hour train journey to Paris was tedious—it really is a very boring journey, so flat and characterless the landscape—and not having a corner seat I could not escape into sleep, and there was anyhow too much conversation in the compartment. I was wedged between a fat, square, masculine middle-aged-to-elderly woman of Semitic appearance, and a trendy young woman. The fat one wore a knitted bobble cap and smoked a cheroot, and volunteered the information that she had gone from Cyprus to 'Israel'—a line of conversation I did not pursue. The young one, who had lank blonde hair and wore high boots, observed to a glamorous female companion that 'Muggers was good in Staggers on the Queen this week', and this I did most eagerly pursue. 'Oh, do tell me !' I exclaimed, and she obligingly handed me the current *New Statesman* to read for myself what Mr. Muggeridge had said about our dear Queen. It proved to be an amusing fantasy about taking Shakespeare round modern London, and how surprised he would be that there was still Queen Elizabeth on the throne, but how it would be explained to him that 'this one was harmless,' and the worst that could be expected would be 'inevitable facetious comments by her consort on public occasions . . .' This, I admit, brightened the dull journey.

The train—the Golden Arrow—trundled round Paris from the Gare du Nord to the Gare de Lyons, where the Simplon Express waited at the other side of the platform, and here I lost both the Staggers girls and the Semitic lady, though I saw the girls later on the train.

There were no porters and but for a helpful young Italian I do not know how I should have got my suitcase up the high steps from the platform into the train. I had forgotten that you don't just get into a Continental train but have to *climb*

into it. When I peered into a compartment with unoccupied
seats a peasant-type woman patted the seat beside her and
smiled an invitation to join her, which I did. She proved to be
Yugoslavian and had virtually no English, so that communication between us had to be by an Esperanto of goodwill, but she
did contrive to convey her nationality to me, and I in turn
somehow made her understand that I had been in Dubrovnik,
Split, and Zagreb, which seemed to delight her. The compartment filled up with a very fat Italian woman, a plump
Greek girl, the young Italian who had helped me, and others
who came and went during the long, hot, hard night. Having
a corner seat I might have slept—I can usually sleep on trains
—but that I had the Greek girl next to me, and she kept
bouncing up to open the window, slide the door, fidget with
her baggage, go out into the corridor, and I conceived a fearful hatred of her. But I was stuck with her in the morning, and
we had coffee and toast together standing up at the buffet bar
on Venice railway station, then walked across Venice together
to St. Mark's, where we parted, and I was blessedly alone.
Come morning I no longer hated her; I even didn't mind her,
but she was of no interest to me, nor I to her. She spoke good
English, but I felt I had had more 'communication' with the
amiable non-English speaking Yugoslavian woman.

From the train there had been orchards of white blossom
during the early morning; then suddenly there was a sheet of
water—the Lido. We reached Venice shortly before nine
o'clock, and a representative of the Greek shipping line met the
train and relieved passengers travelling on that evening by the
ship leaving for Alexandria of their baggage. He also relieved
them of seven hundred lira apiece for transport of their baggage
to the ship. In retrospect it seemed excessive, but at the time it
seemed worth it, for to be free of one's baggage left one splendidly free. The ship did not sail until the evening, and it was
then only nine in the morning. There were eight hours, at
least, in which to rediscover the most beautiful city in the
world.

I recorded in my journal :

'The walk across Venice from the railway station was very
long, but the Greek girl seemed to know her way through the

labyrinth of narrow streets. The walk took a long time because she kept stopping to look in bead shops, saying she had to buy some presents. She had to meet her sister and some friends in the Piazza san Marco, and they were all going on by the steamer in the evening to Athens. She revealed herself as a law student, but she looked such a fat suety lump I'd not have thought her capable of so intellectual a pursuit. She asked me what was my "job", and I told her I was a writer, and that I had an Italian publisher in Milan, but she seemed not much interested. Beads were evidently her preoccupation, and she eventually bought some. When we parted at St. Mark's we said vaguely that we'd meet again in the ship, but in fact we did not.

'In spite of the dawdling and the bead shops I enjoyed strolling in the fresh morning air, and receiving again the tremendous impact of the beauty of Venice. Most wonderful seemed the trafficless peace of the narrow lanes, with only human voices and the sound of footsteps—a sound so unaccustomed it is almost eerie. It is not silence in the Venetian labyrinth but *quietness*—a living quiet made up of small human sounds, the burr of voices, broken occasionally with laughter, and the strange soft shuffle and pat of feet moving on paving stones and steps.

'When I was alone I walked slowly all round the Piazza san Marco, under the arcades, pausing to look at the church from all angles. I felt, as nearly forty years ago, not reconciled to the harshness of the tall brick campanile juxtaposed to the delicate, poetic beauty of the church. How really indescribable is that ethereal beauty! The Byzantine domes, the blues and pinks of the faded murals, the golden mosaics, the winged lions, and those magnificent prancing bronze stallions above the main entrance . . . it is all there before your eyes, yet somehow unbelievable, something in a dream.

'The sun was bright, and tourists with cameras almost as abundant as the pigeons. Too many tourists, too many pigeons, but nothing can diminish that miracle of rare device that is the cathedral church of San Marco.

'I went in, but it seemed very dark after the bright sunlight outside. I peered at the golden mosaics through the gloom, but did not stay long. I had a restless longing to be out in the sunshine, renewing acquaintance with Venice itself.

'A small orchestra was playing at a café on the sunny side of the piazza, and a number of people sat there, at little tables, in the sunshine, but I hankered, nostalgically, for Florian's, on the shady side, and I crossed over and sat there, in the front row, at the edge of the sun.

'I ordered Campari and it was brought to me in a little bottle, Campari-soda, ready mixed, and it was delicious. I ordered a cheese-and-ham sandwich, and later a coffee. I felt very happy. I confided to the waiter that I had not been in Venice for nearly forty years, and everything seemed unchanged. Venice does not change, he said; only the way of life. He had good English and we talked a little. He told me that Florian's was two hundred and forty years old.

'At mid-day there was a commotion of bells. I walked along the waterfront, from the piazza, and found a travel agent's, where I got a map. I then walked westward, determined to find the Maritime station, where the ship would be berthed. Using the map I came to it by way of the Ponte Accademia, which is being reconstructed, which seems a pity, as the old hump-backed wooden bridge is very beautiful.'

From the Accademia bridge you look down the Grand Canal to the domes of the church of Santa Maria della Salute, and there are tall striped poles in the water, and the lovely façades of houses that stand with their feet in the water. I walked along the waterfront to the Santa Maria della Salute, and sat on the steps looking across the canal to the rose-coloured splendour of the Doge's Palace. A little way off a frowsy-looking woman was making a watercolour of the black gondolas and the pink buildings opposite, and it was all somehow curiously E. M. Forster, I recorded in my journal. I went into the church, but it seemed too grand and cold and reminded me of St. Paul's Cathedral, the interior of which I have never liked. I came out and walked all round the church, and an old man in a peaked cap said what I took to mean that it was a beautiful day, so I said yes, it was that, and continued on the long walk to the Terminal, broken at one point by a halt at a waterfront café to eat ice-cream and drink coffee. Some children with fishing nets squatted on the ground with a card-board box containing small live crabs, the legs of which they were breaking off, which seemed to afford them amusement. . . .

I left the café and continued on my way, turning into a narrow lane beside a canal, where I had an impulse to go into a pension and inquire their terms, and learned that in the 'low season', that is to say from November until the end of April, they were thirty-five shillings a day, demi-pension. There were no doubt cheaper pensions, but I wanted an indication. I had a fantasy of returning to Venice in the late autumn or early winter and living and working there. I thought about Frederick Rolfe, 'Baron Corvo', for whose novel, *The Desire and Pursuit of the Whole*, I have so tremendous an admiration, and the setting for which is Venice, and which was written there, and I wondered where was the hotel in which he had lived and died. I saw on the wall of a house near the Santa Maria della Salute a tablet with something about Ruskin, but it was in Italian, and I could not read it. Perhaps, I thought, the time had come to re-read *The Stones of Venice*.

When I finally reached the Maritime Terminal with its many ships, and had satisfied myself that the one for Alex-andria was really there, yellow-funnelled, and carrying a lot of superstructure, as I had been warned in London by the travel agents, so that she rolled in bad weather, and observed that she was getting up steam in readiness to sail that evening, I walked back by the map to the Ponte Accademia and over bridges and along narrow lanes and across wide squares, continually con-sulting the map, and came at last to the Rialto—the most crowded part of Venice, and as noisy as a traffic-ridden street, with the chug of motor-launches and steamers, and their raucous hootings. I was glad to 'stand once more upon the Rialto', but also glad to leave it.

When I left that crowded, noisy area I mooched, no longer walking by the map but turning at random into by-ways, cross-ing hump-backed bridges, losing myself in the labyrinth, but confident of being able to find my way back. At one point I went into a shop and bought a bottle-opener shaped as a sea-horse, a pleasant gilded trifle that cost a thousand lira, then about one pound sterling. There was lovely porcelain and glass in the shop—the lovely Venetian glass—but I could look and delight in it without coveting. I was happy to have just the little sea-horse.

I was altogether very happy during those eight hours in Venice. I got back to the Maritime Terminal in the early evening very tired from all that walking. Very tired but well content to have renewed contact with the wonderful city slowly sinking into the sea. I have never been back; the fantasy faded—it being in the nature of fantasy to do so. I will probably never be in Venice again, but I have been there twice, in youth and in age, and blessed are mine eyes for they have seen. . . .

2

Greek Steamer

In the table-seating arrangements I had asked not to be put
with English people, fearing that being alone I might be
paired-off with—well, almost anyone, but my greatest fear, I
suppose, being of some elderly spinster type in deadly cultural
earnest about Greece. I need not have feared, however, for
there were apparently only two other English passengers in the
first-class, both men, one of them monocled and alcoholic, and
they were paired up. I was put with two married couples—a
German couple from Hamburg, the wife youngish and a fearful synthetic blonde, the man a good bit older, and an amiable
middle-aged French couple; we were six at table with a
staff-captain of heavy, dowager-duchess charm. It was quickly
revealed that the Frenchman knew and liked London and had
a son at London University, and that the German had spent
three years in Scotland as prisoner-of-war—he referred to those
years, from 1943 until August, 1947, as his 'prisonership'. I
came to like the German and the Frenchman very much; the
wives of both were negligible, not contributing much to the
conversation. Of the staff-captain I recorded in my journal that
'he lays the charm on with great elaboration, bowing slightly
to us across the table at the end of dinner, and saying, "Shall
we go now and take coffee?" It is his gracious permission,
as it is not etiquette to rise from the table before he does.' The
other staff-captain invariably came in late to all meals, always
with a party, rather lively, and, I think, all Greeks. But Ger-

mans predominated; there were a few Greeks, a few Italians,
the two Englishmen, the French couple, but the rest of the
passengers seemed to be all German. I recorded: 'There are a
number of very large *Frauen,* all of quite incredible frowsiness.
But there are also a few young and attractive ones.'

I liked it all well enough; I sat in the bar before dinner
drinking Campari; I lay in my cabin reading T. H. White's
book, *The Goshawk,* with a good deal of interest and a slight
disapproval; I typed letters, and my journal. The food was
only so-so, as I had been warned it would be, served lukewarm,
but it was eatable, and I discovered the virtues of Greek
beer.

The first day at sea the day was bright with sunshine, the
sea very blue, and choppy, the wind cold, and no one sat out
on deck, though the German at my table told me at dinner
that he had found a sheltered place for a while 'at the backside
of the ship.' I talked to him in the lounge after dinner, his
wife having gone dancing; he told me that in his Scottish
prisoner-of-war camp they were allowed to send food parcels
to Germany, which some of them did, but, he said, they never
arrived. He had been interested in Victor Gollancz, whom he
referred to as a journalist, who had initiated the sending of
food parcels; he felt that it was a considerable gesture on the
part of one who was a Jew. There were Jewish doctors in the
prison camp, he said, and he had been surprised by the 'anti-
Semitism' he had found amongst British soldiers. He asked me
if when you asked someone how-are-you and they replied not-
too-bad if this was Scottish. . . .

I came to like this German fellow-passenger very much. He
was immensely tall, with a pleasant, intelligent ugly face, and a
good sense of humour. He had noticed that I did not eat meat
and asked was it for 'spiritual' reasons; I said no, ethical, to
which he replied, inevitably, *So!* Thereby relieving me of any
necessity to go into those reasons.

We did all, I suppose, discreetly observe each other. Just as
the German had observed that I did not take meat, so I observed that the Frenchman drank Italian wines. I asked him if he
disliked Greek wines, as I did, and he agreed they needed getting used to. Since he had mentioned that he had been in Alex

many times I asked him if he liked the famous Gianaclis wines from the vineyards there and was astonished to learn that he had never heard of them. I heard him discussing them later with the staff-captain in French and a reference to 'les Arabes', the inflection faintly derogatory.

That first day at sea the ship rolled considerably. By the evening we were off Brindisi, and I wished I had a map. It being cold and uncomfortable on deck I stayed in my cabin reading *The Goshawk*, 'with increasing disapproval,' I wrote in my journal, adding, 'T. H. White was a fine writer, and the book deserves to be the modern classic it is, but why must the wild and free be trapped and tamed to gratify the human lust for power and possession?' I wrote letters for posting when we arrived at Piraeus at noon next day, and learned at dinner that there was to be an organised trip ashore to see the night-life of Athens and *son-et-lumière*. This did not appeal; the *son-et-lumière*, I supposed, would be at the Acropolis, and I had seen it in Cairo, at the Pyramids and Sphinx—so sickening in English that I wished I had settled for it in Arabic, which I wouldn't have understood, but which would at least have sounded melodious and left me free to enjoy the beauty of the *lumière*. What I wanted was to go ashore in daylight, and mooch, in Athens, and on the Acropolis. Putting our watches forward that night there was the feeling, 'It begins to be the East.' Well, the Near East, anyhow.

On the second day we moved through the Greek Islands. I recorded in my journal: 'It was windy and chilly on deck, so I observed the islands through the open doors of the lounge. They were at either side of the ship, steep hills rising directly, it seemed, from the brilliantly blue sea, wooded, and with occasional villages at their feet.' Truth to tell I thought them more beautiful seen from the air when flying over them to Tokyo and Cairo. They become monotonous after a few hours, and I thought of the Greek political prisoners on those islands.

At lunch, that day, the staff-captain addressed himself to me, having learned that I was a writer. He said that he enjoyed meeting writers, and had met Laurence Durrell and Patrick Fermor. In the course of conversation he revealed that he knew England; he had been at Trinity College, Cambridge. It was also revealed that he wrote poetry. He declared that it was good to make sea-voyages because it enabled one to reflect.

After lunch we passed through the very narrow canal of the Isthmus of Corinth, and everyone crowded out on to the deck. We were piloted through this cleft, which is only seventy feet wide, with the rock-faces rising sheer, and only a few feet of water at each side of the ship. For such vessels as can navigate it—it is only twenty-six feet deep—this canal shortens the journey from the Adriatic to Piraeus, the port for Athens, by some two hundred miles. It is about four miles long. We entered it at two o'clock and reached Piraeus at five-thirty, and I went ashore for an hour. The port is about six miles south-west of Athens, with which it forms one continuous urban area. The mass of Athens is clearly visible, crowded at the foot of its mountains, and crowned by the Acropolis, isolated on its hill top in the near-distance. From the harbour I walked across a main street to a broad flight of steps with another main street running along above, leading to a road sloping down to another harbour—the port consists of three harbours. It is from this second harbour that there is the distance view of Athens. Outside a café by this harbour there was a notice: All Kinds of Drinks. Everything else was in Greek. There were little, twisted, mutilated acacia trees lining the streets, and a few palm trees—which somehow surprised me. I came to some public gardens in which I found a Judas tree in full flower, and some very sweet-scented shrubs. I would have liked more than an hour in Piraeus, but dinner was at six-thirty that evening so that the crew could get to Athens, and, as I recorded in my journal, 'the crash-bang in the kitchen, presumably to that end, was terrific.'

3

Athens and the Acropolis

Having learned, the evening before, that there was a sight-
seeing conducted tour in the morning, which would include
the Acropolis, I bought a ticket for it and went ashore at eight
o'clock and crowded with my fellow-passengers into the big
waiting coach. A uniformed young woman took up her position in front of the coach and as we drove out of Piraeus towards Athens addressed us in German. No doubt, I thought,
comfortingly, it would all be repeated in English later; but
it was not, and I felt aggrieved. True, Germans predominated,
but there *were*, after all, other nationalities aboard, dammit.

We disembarked at the foot of the Acropolis hill and I told
the guide that unfortunately her commentary had been lost on
me as I did not understand Deutsch—not all the passengers
are Germans, I pointed out. She regarded me with distaste.

'There is a small 'bus for *non-Germans*,' she said, severely.
Perhaps I 'over-reacted' but it seemed almost as though she
had said for non-whites.

'For this 'bus,' the *Fräulein* continued, 'you should now
wait. It will be arriving with the French people and another
English lady.' (The other English lady was in fact an American
girl.)

I decided, however, not to hang about waiting for those
other lesser breeds without the law, but to 'do' the Acropolis
and explore Athens on my own. Perhaps, even, up at the
Acropolis I might find the *non-German* party. But it was not

important. What was important was that at last, at the age of
sixty-three, I should stand upon the Acropolis. Now that I
was there it seemed somehow strange that I should have left it
until so late in the day. But for so long there had been valid
reasons for not going to Greece; mainly political ones; there
still were. But there was this Greek steamer for Alex, and it
had called there . . .

Well, it would seem that an acropolis is any old citadel on
any old hill, but the Athens one being the most famous has
become *the* Acropolis.

I recorded in my journal: 'I am glad I haven't to write
about the Acropolis because I don't think I would know how
to cope with it!' It is, of course, in a superb setting on its high
hill, with mountains behind, and in the foreground, below,
dark woods of fir and cypress; and then it has the glory of rose-
tinted columns against the brilliant blue of the sky. It is so
absolute in its beauty that there's no way, that I can find, of
serving it with words—not prose, anyhow. One might write a
poem about it, or paint it, if one had the gift to do either,
but in words one can only fall back upon archaeological
description—and I don't know enough, even for that. I can
only catalogue a few of the things I have remembered—a nude
reclining male figure at one end of the Parthenon, under the
marble eaves, and the head of a horse looking out from the
other end—of immense grace, and perfect, that is to say un-
damaged, like the one in the Elgin Marbles collection in the
British Museum. Obviously other figures completed the
frieze. It's all 5th century B.C., which is not so very old com-
pared with Babylon and other archaeological remains in
Iraq, but that so much should have remained intact after two
thousand years and more seems most wonderful. There is a
small temple, with caryatids, and a noble colonnade, and I
wished I had a good English-speaking guide with me, but
preferably an archaeologist, and I wondered what all the
tourists milling about, with their cameras, made of it all.

The Parthenon, the great temple to the goddess Athena,
dominates the Acropolis as the Acropolis dominates Athens.
You may ascend the massive rock platform on which it stands
and walk amongst the wonderful fluted Doric columns. I did

not know at the time but I have learned since that it is considered the most perfect example of the Doric order. Nor did I know at the time that in the 6th century the temple became a church dedicated to St. Sophia, and that in the 15th century, when Athens was captured by the Turks, it became a mosque —not, as Arnold Bennett so astonishingly asserted in his book, *Mediterranean Scenes*,* a Turkish harem. Before I made this visit to Greece I was amongst those who supported the idea, occasionally revived, that the 'Elgin marbles', removed from the Parthenon, should be returned to Greece. Perhaps they should, now, but at the beginning of the 19th century when Lord Elgin obtained permission to make castes and drawings of the Parthenon, sculptures, and to remove certain of them and transport them to England, he would seem to have been carrying out a rescue operation, for ever since the Turks, in 1687, used the temple as a powder magazine during the bombardment of the Acropolis by a Venetian army, and a shell destroyed the middle of the temple, the history of the Parthenon had been one of damage, destruction, and neglect. The 'Elgin marbles' were bought by the British government in 1816 for £30,000, though Elgin himself had spent more than £50,000 on the colection.

I find comfort in the fact that even Arnold Bennett did not know how to describe the Acropolis. He begins his chapter on it, 'The pen hesitates,' and goes on to speak of 'a forest and confusion of marble pillars,' and later of standing 'in the midst of the supreme secular monument of classical antiquity.' He was opposed to the partial restoration of the Parthenon, with outrageous lintels of concrete, and here he had a point, as also, I think, in asserting that 'the Athenians of the fifth century B.C. had no peers in architecture', and demanding, 'Why seek vainly to re-create a vanished enchantment?'

But on all this I had no views the morning I wandered amongst the fluted columns and gazed at broken sculptures and damaged friezes of incredible beauty. I knew almost nothing about any of it, but I stood at last upon the Acropolis, and as in Venice the milling tourists could not diminish the tremendous impact of a miraculous beauty. The tourists

* 1928.

Guard at the Royal Palace, Athens—'apparently oblivious of the tourists who stare at him and photograph him as though he were an animal in a zoo . . .'

House of Commons, 1969. At a press conference for the release of Greek women political prisoners: Dame Peggy Ashcroft; Anne Kerr, M.P.; the author; and Betty Ambatielos

Rhodes: The Castle of the Knights

seemed to swarm like ants—or the pigeons in the *piazza* of San
Marco; at times it was quite difficult to escape the line-of-fire
of cameras, all busily recording in colour the gleaming columns
against the deep blue sky, and there was, also, an infestation of
street photographers, persistently pestering. So thick on the
ground were the tourists and the photographers that it could
almost be said that there was standing-room only on the
Acropolis.

Arnold Bennett had assured me, back in the twenties, that as
I liked Paris I would like Athens, and visiting the Greek
capital nearly thirty-five years later I remembered this, and it
seemed strange to me that Bennett, who knew Paris, could have
said it, for I found no slightest affinity between the two cities.
I had thought Athens curiously arid when we had driven
through it, and from the Parthenon, from which it is to be seen
sprawling immensely in the valley and climbing the hillsides in
a grey density, it looked ugly. Later, wandering in the wide
streets, I realised that there were many handsome buildings,
pillared and imposing, and boulevards flanked by acacia trees,
and some broad squares with bright flower beds, and trees, but
for me the overall impression was of a grey-white, yellowish-
white, aridity, and in recent years it has been something of a
relief to hear it quite commonly asserted that Athens is an
unattractive city. But one thing I did like, and that was the
fine National Park with its tall trees, and a lovely wistaria
arbour hung with thick pendants of blossom, reminding me of
so many beautiful parks in Japan. At the entrance to the
Athens park there is a marble monument to Byron. It shows
him being crowned by Hellas, a buxom female naked to the
waist, Byron cloaked and booted, and both perched on a pede-
stal at the top of a flight of steps, and all singularly silly; which
is a pity.

I was in the Park only briefly, with a little time in hand
before the 'bus left for Piraeus, but before then I had seen
the outside of the Royal Palace in the company of a middle-
aged Swiss woman who had attached herself to me at the
Acropolis, and with her, also, I saw the vast stadium, built in
1896, where the first revived Olympic games were played; it

H

is reputed to hold 70,000 people. Of the Royal Palace my most vivid memory is of a young sentry standing rigidly and expressionless at the gates, like a dummy, in his curious uniform of tight white breeches and red and blue tunic, apparently oblivious of the tourists who stared at him and photographed him as though he were an animal in a zoo rather than a fellow human being. I recorded in my journal that the Swiss woman wondered what he thought in the face of all that, and that I replied that he probably didn't think, but simply accepted it all as part of the tedium of sentry-go.

On the return journey to Piraeus—in the *small* 'bus, for *non*-Germans, I discovered that the port has a third harbour—the small harbour of its famous Yacht Club.

We reached the ship to find a crowd of women wearing black robes and head-scarves struggling up the gangways with bundles and baskets. They appeared to be peasants, with gaunt, seamed faces, and most of them old. Abroad many were already squatting on the bare boards of the lower deck amongst their bundles, in the Eastern manner. There were also a number of Orthodox priests aboard, all long hair and high hats and thick black beards, but these were in the first-class. . . .

I inquired of an amiable Cypriot who had come aboard, and with whom I got into conversation, leaning against the rail as we steamed out of Piraeus, who were all those black-robed women, and why this influx of priests. He explained that they were pilgrims going to Jerusalem for the Orthodox Easter. There, he said, they would wear white. He pointed out that though the pilgrims were predominantly women there were also a few old men; also that they were not all travelling 'deck'—there were a few in the second-class, and some in the first. Later I noticed some of them, wearing large coloured medallions on their chests depicting the head of Jesus crowned with thorns, and among them a very old couple, a man and a woman, who looked as though they were at death's door and going to Jerusalem to die—and perhaps they were, as Hindus go to Benares whilst they still have strength for the journey.

I found the Cypriot intelligent and interesting and we talked a good deal together, mostly about the Cyprus problem, very much an issue at that time. He had very good English, and a political sophistication in relation to Middle East affairs, coupled with ease of manner, that made conversation with him very congenial. He was interested in a copy of *A Lance for the Arabs* I was taking with me to Cairo and urged that I should come to Cyprus and write a book about it in the way I had written about the Arab countries—that is to say a travel book which would also present the political situation. He could arrange facilities for me with the Ministry of Information, and I would find a great deal of beauty and interest in the island, and it would be arranged for me to meet President Makarios.

I said, evasively, that I didn't know whether the British public would be interested in such a book at this time; that the political situation was so very complicated . . .

'Think about it!' he urged.

I promised to think about it, but all I could think about just then was that tomorrow we were to have a little time ashore at Rhodes, reputedly the most beautiful of all the Greek islands.

4

A Glimpse of Rhodes

There were two newcomers at our table at dinner that evening, a French couple, friends of the staff-captain, who stood us a bottle of Greek wine in celebration, but as there were nine of us—the original French couple, the German couple, plus the new French couple, and the Cypriot and me, and the staff-captain himself, it amounted only to a taste each. Nobody ordered more, and it would have been tactless, I suppose, to have done so, discourteous to our host . . . who was perhaps absent-minded rather than parsimonious.

At the end of the meal—during most of which the Cypriot resumed with me discussion of the Cyprus Problem—we adjourned to the lounge for coffee, but almost immediately the staff-captain was called away by the news brought to him that about a hundred of the pilgrims had no berths and were settling down on the deck for the night and he was concerned to provide shelter for them—awnings, at least, should be rigged up, he considered, even though many of them reckoned to travel 'deck', bringing their own food and camping out on deck, in the Eastern manner, taking a chance with the elements.

There was dancing, and the Cypriot invited me, but I told him my dancing days were over and that I now regarded it as a somewhat curious pastime—and the German laughed and agreed. The Cypriot then went on the dance floor with the Gnädigefrau, and after that, when she was claimed from time to time by others, danced with a lumpy Dutch girl who was some sort of courier in the ship, and the German and I talked. We talked about the war-criminals' trials then proceeding in Germany, which he described as 'cannibalism—German eating German!' The Nuremberg trials, he said, coming from other countries, were a different matter. I agreed about the German trials, but had been opposed to the Nuremberg trials, I told him. So we talked, and watched the dancing, and the others came and went, changing partners. The German danced once or twice, stiffly, with his wife, who looked excruciatingly bored during each performance, in marked contrast with her vivacity with other partners.

The staff-captain did not rejoin us, and by half-past eleven I felt I had had enough of watching couples shuffling round the tiny floor, and I would need to be up early in the morning to get my landing permit for the shore-excursion for the island of Rhodes for which I had booked, and which was scheduled to leave at seven-forty-five.

I breakfasted with the Cypriot at seven, and had hoped to see the German couple again to say goodbye, as they were leaving the ship at Rhodes, but they were not there, and I was sorry; I had liked him; with her I had made no contact at all. I left my card for them, wishing them *bon voyage*, with the Cypriot, who was staying aboard. There was a great crowdedness and confusion in the second-class, with people assembling for the excursion, and others leaving the ship. Finally, half an hour after the scheduled time, the launch left, packed with the pilgrims.

From the ship Rhodes did not present itself as the wild, beautiful island I had expected, but across the harbour a walled city was visible, and a massive castle I understood was the fortress of the Knights Hospitallers of St. John of Jerusalem, who conquered the island in 1309; this looked interesting, the ancient acropolis, but all down below, modern Rhodes, was a density of modern blocks—there were sixty hotels in this new part,* the guide in charge of the excursion told us, and tourism was the chief industry.

We went ashore from the launch and piled into waiting coaches, and I recorded in my journal :

* There are twice that number today.

'A motor road winds up the hillside, zigzagging like the Corniche roads in the south of France, and there are umbrella-pines and eucalyptus adding to this Riviera effect. There are what the guide called some "ruins of Apollo", a few pillars, presumably of a temple, standing out in the open, unprotected, and similar other Greek oddments. We came by this long way round to the Castle and the old city, reminiscent of Carcassonne with its walls and narrow, sharply cobbled streets and medieval houses, some of which are very beautiful. It seems at first incredible, as at Carcassonne, that people still live in this medieval setting, but there were glimpses of inner courtyards, with fig trees, and washing hanging out, and cats sunning themselves, and we passed a school, clamorous with children at play in the courtyard in front of it.

'At the Castle of the Knights there were rooms with walls of bare stone, and mosaic floors, and burial urns, and fragments of ancient pottery, but it was all too cursory a view, with the guide gabbling first in Greek to the pilgrims, and then very briefly to the "English people", who consisted of an American girl, a Swiss woman, and myself. It all added up to the merest glimpse, and as the American girl observed to me, as we zig-zagged in the coach down to the harbour where the launch waited to take us back to the ship, it was "very frustrating".

'Behind the old city, inland, rise high mountains; somewhere in there lies the "valley of butterflies". . . .

'We were back in the ship by ten, and sailed at one sharp.

'I sat in the lounge for a time with the American girl, giving her useful hints about Cairo, and she in turn telling me about Washington D.C., to which I was flying within a few days of my return from Cairo, as the guest of a group of young Arab diplomats who wished to celebrate the American publication of *The Road to Beersheba* with a reception for its author. I would like Washington, she assured me, it was a fine city, and I would like the flight—about which I had expressed apprehension, never having flown the Atlantic before—for, said she, "they get you half drunk and everyone is very gay, but," she added, "if you don't like it that way you can always take a tranquilliser. . . ." I declared that I would take it neat—fear, claustrophobia and all, and the drinks had better be good.

'At lunch there were two more French people, and wine stood for all of us by the newcomers—I don't know how many bottles, but glasses were continually recharged. Coffee in the lounge, and finally the staff-captain and I were left alone and talked of *maya* and the illusion of the "appearances of reality", and of inner loneliness, and the apartness of the artist . . . after which uplifting discourse I retired to my cabin to pack and make up my journal.

'The ship is restless with impending departures. Have I enjoyed the trip? I think I have not minded it rather than positively enjoyed it, and I am glad to be leaving the ship tomorrow, for I've had enough of it, and the pilgrims, with Jesus pinned to their bosoms, and yellow death in some of their old, lined faces, have brought a Lourdes atmosphere aboard, and the Greek Orthodox priests, with their high hats and thick beards and black robes and grey hair knotted into buns, give me the creeps. . . .

'I am glad to have stood at last upon the Acropolis, and seen something of Athens and Piraeus, and had at least a glimpse of Rhodes. Odd that I never saw again the Greek girl with whom I trekked across Venice. I have enjoyed talking with the so-literary Greek staff-captain, and the so-political Cypriot, and the amiable German with his pleasant Fernandel ugliness.

'Tomorrow Alex, and Greek-Egyptian friends, the amusing Tanashi and the lovely Helene, and the delicious Gianaclis wines.

'It will be Bairam, the Muslim Christmas, and the streets will throng with children in their bright new Bairam dresses, crude pinks and harsh reds, and they will be riding in carriages, drawn by lean horses, spending the money given them for Bairam, and there will be a salvo of twenty-one guns across the bay.'

We berthed at nine-thirty in the morning. There was a hot high wind blowing, the kamseen, the desert wind. Tanashi and Helene were at the quayside, and to my surprise and pleasure, Adel Amin, who had come up from Cairo the day before.

There was lunch at the Sporting Club, and then we saw

Adel off on the afternoon train back to Cairo. In the evening there was the Greek Club, then dinner at a Greek restaurant where Italian young men sang Greek songs. The Greek steamer had berthed at Alex, but somehow it was still Greece.

On my third day in Alex I saw an Egyptian English-language newspaper, the *Egyptian Mail*, in which I read that I had arrived in Cairo yesterday on a four-day visit.

PART IV

Paris Interlude, 1971

After my visit to Syria in the autumn of 1966 I did not leave England again until June, 1971, when I went to Paris for a reunion with my old friend, Rickey Austin, whom I had not seen since the spring of 1966, when I did my 'American journey' from New York to Los Angeles by Greyhound, about which I have written elsewhere.*

When I did that heroic journey Rickey and I had not met for about fifteen years, though we had most steadfastly corresponded; the Paris reunion, therefore, after an interval of only five years, was a relatively minor affair. The reunion, for me, was really with Paris—this time it was Paris I had not seen for about fifteen years.

England was not in Rickey's itinerary, though he had been prepared to come to London had I been unable to go to Paris. We were agreed that we would prefer to meet in Paris, a city we both find more simpatico. I accordingly made the effort and up-and-went, by boat and train, via Boulogne. The 'effort' was necessary because I had not been feeling well for some time, and also because I had lost the habit of foreign travel, and not travelling can become as much a habit as travel itself.

I went by boat and train because after an enormous amount of flying—including to the Far East, U.S.A., Russia, and all over the Middle East—I have come to detest this form of

* *An American Journey*, 1967.

transport. It is not travel—it is merely transport; and boring to a degree which after a great deal of it becomes unbearable —apart from the claustrophobia, the frightful 'plastic' meals, and the excruciating ear-ache which can happen on descents. But mostly—anyhow for me—the case against it is the sheer boredom. Journeying by train and boat is interesting, even a little of an adventure. But then I like trains and ships, and 'give me terra firma—no matter how infirma', as a friend of mine, who also dislikes air-travel, likes to say.

So I booked myself from Victoria, via Boulogne, which takes a little longer but is also a little cheaper than Dover–Calais, which used to be the 'posh' route, by Golden Arrow, with its French counterpart, the Flêche D'Or, waiting at the other side. Both these great, romantic trains existed at the time, but as I write this, just over a year later, are no more. The Golden Arrow, creaking at the joints, it would seem, has pulled into Victoria for the last time. Had I known this was to happen I might have gone by the Golden Arrow for the farewell; but as it was I was happy to be on the boat-train for Folkestone, and looking forward to the Channel crossing.

But disillusion set early in. At Victoria there was a discouraging notice that due to a 'partial strike' in Paris trains 'may be subject to delay.' The Channel crossing was a shock. In the old days, even as late as the fifties, by whatever route it was *fun*; you lingered on deck for a bit, perhaps, permitting yourself to be a little sentimental about the receding white cliffs of old England, then went below to the bar and reached France all too soon—even by Dieppe, the long route. It was all very civilised, sophisticated—rakish, even. I have no idea when it stopped being like that; I can only record that it is not like that now. What-it-is-like-now is a babbling mass of groups and parties of people who are not bôna-fide travellers but impersonalised persons being packaged from one place to another. A lost-looking, hippie-style young man and I appeared to be the only independent passengers. There were a great many Americans and Germans, and if one lot was noisier than the other it was the other, though the Germans, I think, won by a short head. There was no place to hide; no quiet corner in any lounge or bar. In the buffet I heard a middle-aged American ask for some ice for his hot coffee—'take the burn out of it,' he explained. The waiter impassively doled out some ice cubes. 'That's right,' he said, soothingly, as though dealing with a harmless lunatic, 'you take the burn out of it.'

We reached Boulogne to find the scheduled train not running, and we were taken by 'bus to Boulogne ville, where we waited for half an hour in a big empty hall, without seats; finally we were admitted to a platform where we waited for another half-hour, in a cold wind. When at last a train came in it was a struggle to board it; there was no question of getting into a first-class coach because you had a first-class ticket; you were lucky to get into the train at all. I was fortunate to be able to place one buttock on a corner of a seat in a hot, crowded, smoky second-class compartment in which people were standing, and the train trundled across the flat French countryside —an interminable and boring journey at best—and arrived at the Gare du Nord an hour late.

Whilst struggling towards the exit in the crowded corridor I saw Rickey's slim, trim figure charging up the platform to the rear of the train and the first-class coaches. We found each other, eventually, of course, to our intense mutual relief, and taxied across Paris to the Left Bank, to the rue Cassette, close to the Luxembourg Gardens, and a small, old-fashioned, and very good hotel which has remained blessedly unchanged down through the years. Rickey had stayed there for long periods in the past and it would not occur to him to stay anywhere else.

I found a bottle of Bourbon in my room, and after a drink and shower the evils of the journey receded, leaving only the happy, excited awareness that it was Paris again, with the remembered sights and smells and sounds unchanged. In one's youth Paris with a lover, naturally and of course; but in one's age simply to be there with an old and dear friend is happiness enough. Old friends make no demands of each other; they accept each other—warts and all. There are not many advantages in growing old, that I can see, but that capacity for affectionate acceptance seems to me to be one of them. Though, to be sure, there was always between Rickey and me an affectionate, amused tolerance, coupled with a considerable mutual admiration and respect. Down through the years we have stood for the same ideas, championed the same causes, admired—and despised—the same authors.

So there we were again after a brief five years, and there I was again in Paris after fifteen, and Rickey had changed not at all, of course, and Paris—well, not too badly; it could have been worse. That massive high-rise block at the Gare Montparnasse is pretty bad, and it was a shock to be confronted with Drugstore Café across from the old Café des Deux Magots on the Boulevard St. Germain. But still, counting one's blessings, quite a lot is still where one had left it—all those years ago. Most of it, really—of what was important to my generation. The Coupole, the Dome, and the Rotonde across the road from them, up on the Boulevard Montparnasse—old haunts, almost homes from homes, for those of us who were young in the thirties, and full of memories. Of the Dome, particularly, perhaps, for so many writers and artists went there, English and Americans . . . in the old days, between the two world wars.

We walked round to the Boulevard St. Germain, to St. Germain-des-Prés, where the sombre old church is—and the Café des Deux Magots. We did not, that first evening, sit at the Deux Magots, but at a small café with a glass-enclosed terrace, and Rickey drank vodka and I drank whisky, and the traffic flowed past, up and down the boulevard, and the crowds along the pavement. We dined at a small restaurant nearby, but I do not remember what we ate or drank, for tiredness closed in on me; it was lovely to be there, but it had been a long day's journey into that Parisian night. . . .

At the hotel Rickey asked, as we collected our keys, 'What time in the morning?'

'Oh, around nine, I suppose,' I said, carelessly.

He recoiled in horror.

'For God's *sake* !' he exclaimed.

'What, then?' I inquired.

'Not a minute before twelve,' he said, firmly.

'O.K.,' I said, 'I'll knock on your door at noon.'

After *café-complet* in my room at nine I got out at about ten

and walked all through the Luxembourg Gardens to the far
end, coming out at the Observatoire. I walked with a curious
sense of unreality. It all belonged so essentially to my youth. I
was a ghost walking. The narrow avenues of the tall chestnut
trees were dark, the trees in mid-June already heavy with
summer. It was all much the same as when I had last walked
there, in the fifties, except that the little twisted hawthorn trees
on the terrace were gone, replaced by oleanders in tubs. The
little twisted hawthorn trees that had sheltered so many lovers
—they died, I suppose; after all, nothing lasts forever. . . .

Out at the Observatoire the chestnut trees were as thick and
tall and dark as I had remembered, but the old house in the
rue Cassini in which I had done so much work in the thirties
was shabby and rundown, paint and plaster peeling, and some
modern flats had been built next to it. I went into the garden,
past the concierge's lodge, and up the steps and peered in
through the glass doors—through which I had so often passed
into an elegant, well-groomed interior; but all was now shabby
and neglected—scruffy. I felt quite extraordinarily upset. I
had had a charming room in that house, with a divan bed and
bookshelves, and I had enjoyed working there, looking out
into the chestnut trees, so pleasantly close to the quiet, narrow
house, with its grey shutters.

Well, but that had been in the early thirties; it was now
the seventies; it was all, now, nearly forty years ago, more than
half a lifetime.

I turned my back on the Observatoire, and the narrow rue
Cassini, and retraced my steps to the Luxembourg, noting that
the Café de Lilas was still there, with a terrace full of tall
green jungly plants, and continued on down the Boul' Mich' to
the river. The noise was fearful, the whole length of the
boulevard packed with cars, so dense it would have been possible to have walked along their roof tops; cars, cars, cars; I
felt I had never seen so many cars. At the end of the boulevard
I crossed to the other side and walked back to the Luxembourg,
noting with satisfaction that the bookshops I had remembered
were still there, and that great emporium the *100,000
Chemises.*

I got back to the hotel shortly before noon and knocked on

Rickey's door, but did not stay for an answer. He emerged a few minutes later, a little grey in the face, but neat, trim as ever, and trusting I had slept well. We walked a short distance to a *bistro* on the Vaugirard, and drank an aperitif and ate a *plat du jour*, not talking much, there being a tacit understanding between us that talk belongs to the night—the day being an uphill climb to that end. I wrote some postcards, and Rickey smoked and brooded and recovered from the night. After coffee we decided to go to Notre Dame and walk round the island.

We went by taxi because the wind was cold and Rickey was still building up strength.

Notre Dame was all splendidly cleaned, and milling with tourists, inside and out, and a car park was being made in front of it. We walked all round the Île St. Louis and over the Pont Neuf. A motorway has been built on the right bank, and a tall tower dominates the skyline towards the Etoile, spoiling the view, but I found myself unable to agree with a correspondent in *The Times* recently that skyscrapers ruin the view in all directions. This seemed to both of us a gross exaggeration. At that time, June, 1971, Paris had most remarkably escaped the high-rise horror which has ravaged London . . . though since then the right bank has become, alas, to some extent at least, what *The Times,* with accompanying grim photograph, has called Manhattan sur Seine.

Wearying of walking in the cold wind and the greyness we took a taxi up to the Arc de Triomphe, to see what was going on up there, and which proved to be the beginning of that high-rise development which has recently caused so much angry protest (but upon which President Pompidou has set the seal of his approval), and then, because it was cosy in the taxi and windy and cold outside decided to stay put and drive through the Bois.

We were fortunate in having a very pleasant and intelligent young taxi-driver, with whom Rickey chatted in French, and who confirmed what Rickey had already told me—that all but a few of the *pissoirs* which had always been so much a part of the Paris street scene had been abolished, because of *les pédérastes.* He considered it a disgraceful thing that certain

The Byron Monument at the National Park, Athens

'To Paris in June, 1971, to meet my old friend Rickey Austin, whom I had not seen for five years . . .'

'The old house in the rue Cassini, where I had done so much work in the 1930s, and had not seen for fifteen years . . .'

people should behave in such a way as to cause inconvenience
to others. It was also *un peu dégôutant, vous savez.* It was not
the *pédérastes* who needed the *pissoirs*, but taxi drivers, and
old men with kidney troubles. ...

It was pleasant driving slowly through the Bois, along the
lake and through the wooded avenues, and with the high-rise
blocks out of sight it was all as one had remembered it. At the
Café Alexandre, on the Champs Elysées, we said goodbye to
our nice young driver, and he said that it had been a pleasure
driving us. It was quiet at the Alexandre; just a few rather
rich-looking people sedately taking tea in a sedately elegant,
old-fashioned, and expensive atmosphere, squeezing lemon between tongs into thin shallow cups, delicately forking pastries,
and such conversation as there was no more than a well-bred
murmur. Left to myself I might have preferred somewhere
less well-bred and more lively, but the June day was grey and
cold, a day to be enclosed and cosy, the mood subdued, in a
minor key.

When we had taken tea we strolled down the Champs
Elysées, looking in at the windows of art galleries, lingering
once over a painting concerning which Rickey had two minds,
and finally hailing another taxi and returning to the Left Bank
across the gilded splendour of the Pont Alexandre—florid and
vulgar, I suppose, yet somehow magnificent, if only in its
absurdity. Rickey declared that its vulgarity had to be seen to be
believed, but I don't know. ...

Back at the hotel each child withdrew to its room and
rested, and this child stood on its balcony for a while and looked
across the playground of a school to the Eiffel Tower, dark
against an apricot evening sky, and listened to the shrill
sounds of Paris down below, and smelled the strong, pungent
smell of Paris, compact of Gauloise cigarettes, garlic, coffee,
drains, and felt an overwhelming happiness; just to *be* there
—once more—after all those years—and perhaps for the last
time. ...

We emerged from our rooms, as agreed, at the aperitif hour,
six o'clock, and descended to the small lounge and came out
into the narrow rue Cassette and made our way to St.
Germain-des-Prés and the Café des Deux Magots. We went

I

there, I suppose, for old time's sake, for it was always a dullish café, though certain literary lights and a few painters used to go there, deviating from livelier Montparnasse, with the Coupole and the Dome; the Flore, next door to the Magots, was more amusing, but in the thirties was somewhat over-popular with 'queers'. In June, 1971, the old Deux Magots —still with its grotesque painted statues of Gog and Magog— was not quiet and dull but noisy and crowded, and where the artists and writers go now I do not know, but I cannot believe they go there. It was no longer for us, and we recognised and acknowledged the fact immediately, and after one drink each walked out into the boulevard and round the corner to a restaurant 'the type I am liking', as Damon Runyon used to say, all brown panelling and thick net curtains, and quietness, and good food, uncrowded, and tables far apart. I remember only that we began with fat green asparagus, and that it was all fine, splendid, lovely—the food, the wine, and just *being* there.

Back on the Boulevard St. Germain, later, the police were thick on the ground, some with guns on their backs, and how could the students not resent the police out in force like that, when there were no demos? 'Sheer provocation,' we said, and felt angry.

We looked in at a night place run by two American homo-sexual friends of Rickey's. It was half-empty, and therefore dreary. When I was last there it had been packed—one of those hot, crowded, smoky *boîtes* that were quite horrible, really, but to which we all went because everyone else did, though the cost of the drinks was exorbitant, the entertain-ment inferior, and the space on the dance floor about one square foot per person. But you saw 'everyone' there, that is to say a few people you knew, and it was considered 'amusing'.

Rickey and I did not go to this particular night spot because we thought it amusing or expected to meet there anyone we knew, but simply because the couple who ran it were friends of his, and he had been seeing them and had said he would bring me in. They professed to remember me, from the fifties; perhaps they did; it is immaterial. One of them, astonishingly,

mentioned *Confessions and Impressions*—published in 1930!
—as though to demonstrate that he knew something about me
as a writer. But there was tension between the two of them and
it was not easy; one was surly with Rickey, as though accusing
him of taking sides. They were breaking up, Rickey said, and
the break-up was reflected in the place, which was no longer
successful. Each in turn sang songs—of the 'folk-lorish' kind,
and one accompanied himself on a guitar the while. It was
all right and produced some mild applause, but it all lacked
verve, and seemed, in fact, all rather old-hat. There was the
feeling that they sang because the entertainment was included
in the price of the drinks, rather than as in the old days to
create an atmosphere which they enjoyed creating. We sat up
at the bar and Rickey tried to make conversation; one of them
was offhand and unresponsive—the aggrieved one, I supposed; when an *affaire* breaks up there is always an aggrieved
one, hetero or homo. The thing was that they were neither
of them young any more; one of them would go back to the
U.S.A., Rickey thought, and the other—the aggrieved one—
probably just drift along in Paris, getting a job in some bar
or other; perhaps, even, he would form another relationship
—he was, after all, still attractive, in his heavy, sultry fashion.
Rickey wasn't taking sides; relationships do, after all, come to
an end, and this one had been going on for about fifteen years;
and when they do there is always someone who breaks it up,
and someone who cries. Hetero or homo, it's the way it is.

True enough, but it was oppressive, and when a tourist
party came in we took the opportunity to leave. We strolled
back to the Boulevard St. Germain, where the police still
patrolled or stood about in twos and threes, and young men,
as thick on the ground as the *flics,* also stood about in groups,
or promenaded, watching from the sidelines.

Rickey approached a group and asked them why so many
flics, why the *gendarmes mobiles,* with their rifles, when there
was no demo? They laughed, shrugged. No demo was planned, they said, but the police were always expecting trouble,
since May, 1968; they regarded their presence as necessary
to prevent it. They laughed. We were glad they laughed, but
we ourselves felt only anger. That Paris, of all cities, should be

like this, black with police! It was worse than the skyscrapers and the abolition of the *pissoirs*; we made a joke of it because the alternative was to fret and fume with indignation.

But it was a relief to get back to the narrow rue Cassette, silent and empty and unconcerned.

The Gare du Nord in the morning was strikebound and desolate. A few passengers wandered about, gazing disconsolately at empty tracks beyond the ticket barriers. No train departures were indicated, for the good reason that there were no trains to depart. The only life was in the buffet, where people sat at tables, their suitcases at their feet, drank coffees, did a little eating, and waited for a train to be announced or indicated. Rickey and I, after a preliminary skirmish in search of information, joined these passengers-in-waiting—it was at least bright and warm in the buffet, and singularly cold and bleak outside.

There was a continual peering through the plate glass in the hope of sighting a train, and every now and then someone would go out and reconnoitre. A porter trekking across the wide open space of the concourse excited hopes and he was immediately besieged by inquirers. The spectacle had an unsettling effect on those of us still seated in the buffet. There was a snapping of fingers, a summoning of waiters, a calling for *l'addition*, a general movement of departure. Some telephoning from the hotel, earlier, had elicited the information that there was going to be a train during the morning for Boulogne, but no departure time could be given for it. The obvious thing had seemed to be to arrive at the station at the time it would normally leave, then hang around and hope, and this we, and many other people, did; we arrived, that is to say, some time before eleven—and some time around noon a train, almost unbelievably, pulled in.

It was a relief, but it was also a panicky thing. This was it, then—goodbye. Departure; and probably no return. After a few days more in Paris, arranging for the shipment to America of the paintings he had bought, Rickey would return to his home in California; and by that evening, all being well, I should be in my home in London. There would be frequent

letters, as there had always been, down through the years—
some forty odd years, now—and it was not impossible we
should meet again, but it was improbable. Rickey had talked
vaguely about possibly returning to Europe in the 'fall'; it was
a nice idea, but also a kind of whistling in the dark. That
bleak morning on the strike-bound Gare du Nord I don't think
we either of us believed in it. It was a grey day, and I think
we both felt cold and grey; we are neither of us, anyhow, con-
versational in the mornings; we parted, I think greyly;
bleakly. It had been a good brief interlude—too brief; but
something is always better than nothing. And that is not being
ungrateful, but, on the contrary, deeply thankful; contact had
been re-established, friendship and affection re-affirmed—and
I had got back to Paris just in time, before Monsieur Le
President, 'may God forgive him, for I never shall,' sanctioned
the uglification of the world's most beautiful capital city, and
his Prime Minister, Monsieur Pierre Messmer, had declared,
in the debate over the skyscrapers to the west of the Arc de
Triomphe, that every period should bring its contribution to
the architecture of Paris, and that there could be 'no question
of freezing the development of the capital out of respect for
the past alone.'* Someone should perhaps explain to both
gentlemen that skycrapers are not 'architecture'. . . .

* *The Times,* October 2, 1972, Patrick Brogan reporting from Paris,
October.

PART V

England

My Burglar, Mr. Stanley

To the police, with whom he had been closely associated since the age of fourteen, he was Frank Stanley. Frank Arthur Stanley. To Reginald and me he was never anything but Mr. Stanley. Reginald, who was normally very free with first names, was very strict about it. He defended Stanley in court, visited him in prison, wrote to him, was sympathetic to him—though it was he, Reginald, who had suffered when Stanley burgled Oak Cottage—but he resolutely opposed first-name intimacy. He explained to me, once, 'I don't want him calling me Reg so I can't call him Frank.' Why he who was 'Reg' to everyone almost from the word go didn't want the same familiarity with Stanley is an interesting psychological point. Something to do with an only half-suppressed resentment, perhaps; or perhaps simply that despite our friendliness towards Stanley we neither of us managed to like him very much. It was not that we *dis*liked him, and certainly we were sympathetic to him, but, also, we were not drawn to him. Reginald was amused by him, up to a point, and I was interested in him—as a human problem—but only up to a point. So that from first to last—and it covered a period of about ten years —he remained, Mr. Stanley.

Reginald wrote about him, with humour and sympathy, in his autobiography, *My Life and Crimes,* published in 1956, two years before his death, and whilst Stanley was only at the beginning of the seven years' Preventive Detention he was given following his Oak Cottage escapade, despite Reginald's efforts on his behalf. Reginald was in court at Stanley's trial, at the Quarter Sessions, as a witness, and was allowed by Tudor Rees, the Chairman, to speak in his defence. When Reginald stepped down the Chairman said such kind things about him, and about the Society of Friends in general—duly reported in the press as 'Judge compliments Quaker who turned the other cheek'—that it was a shock when he came to deal with the prisoner that he addressed him sternly, declaring that he had had a 'record of felony' from the age of fourteen. At that Mr. Stanley protested: 'Excuse me, sir, that's not correct.' This produced in court what Reginald described as a 'terrifying silence', and then Tudor Rees said, 'in a calm, quiet voice, "Proceed, Stanley." ' Mr. Stanley then proceeded:

'At the age of fourteen, sir, I was sent to an Approved School for travelling in a train without a ticket—a thing, sir, which you or anyone else might have done.'

Reginald wrote that he again held his breath, 'in what seemed a loaded silence. The Chairman said nothing, shuffled some papers, and was handed others before he spoke again.

'Yes,' he said, mildly, 'that's true.'

He made a comment on the severity with which Mr. Stanley had been treated in his youth. He surveyed his career slowly and carefully, pausing sometimes to murmur something in criticism of past sentences. . . . But he ended by giving him 'seven years' preventive detention'.

Reginald was horrified, but Stanley later assured him that he was sure it would have been an even heavier sentence, 'but for you turning up to speak for me.'

We both visited him, in due course, in Parkhurst prison, to which he returned rather as one returning to a familiar hotel, and hoping to get his old room back, which I believe he did. He always had a cell to himself; he was a model prisoner, and what might be called a Parkhurst Old Hand, and to some extent privileged.

The Parkhurst visit was made in June, 1958, just six months before Reginald's sudden death from a cerebral haemorrhage whilst in Australia on a lecture tour for the Quakers. Of all this I have written in *Brief Voices,* a volume of autobiography published in 1959, and which records his death.

I kept in touch with Stanley, sending him books and magazines and writing to him, because I knew that Reginald would have done so, and I met him in London soon after the expiration of his sentence. We met at Waterloo station and took a taxi to Scotland Yard where he had to collect some of his possessions. It was a big moment when we arrived, and, not knowing where to go, a policeman politely inquired, 'Can I help you, sir?'

Stanley turned to me, beaming, as we continued on in the indicated direction. 'Did you hear that?' he demanded. 'He called me *sir*!'

When we had finished with Scotland Yard we travelled out to Wimbledon by train for tea at Oak Cottage.

I said, as I inserted the key in the front door, 'Nice that you're coming in through the front door this time, and by invitation!'

In the sitting-room he went straight to the window and looked out across the lily pond to the rose garden.

'I liked this garden the first time I saw it,' he said appreciatively.

'How could you see the garden then?' I asked. 'In the dark...'

He regarded me with some astonishment.

'We don't do our jobs at *night*,' he said. 'We work in the daytime. It would look suspicious to be seen carrying a suitcase at night! I was here in the afternoon.'

He turned back to the garden.

'It's nice,' he said, and then, 'Who lives up there?' indicating a house above me, just visible through the trees.

'No one very much,' I told him, guardedly. 'Just ordinary middle-class people. Why?'

'I thought of doing that place instead of here.'

'Why didn't you?' I inquired.

'This looked easier.'

'You didn't find much. Only Mr. Reynolds' one good suit and his winter overcoat and some old shirts. No furs or jewellery or silver. Just a lot of books.'

He said warmly, 'As I told Mr. Reynolds, if I'd known it was an author's house I would have refrained.'

He had used that word, 'refrained', in the letter he wrote to Reginald from Brixton prison, whilst he was awaiting trial—he was not granted bail—and he used it again then. I remember this window-seat conversation very vividly.

In the letter from Brixton he had apologised to Reginald 'for all the trouble and expense I have caused you,' and added, 'Had I known I was encroaching on the preserves of a fellow author I would most certainly have refrained.'

'Encroaching on the preserves' seemed a singular euphemism for what the police called, more pointedly, 'breaking and entering.' But since in 1938, at the age of thirty-six, he had published a book, entitled *A Happy Fortnight*, for which Sir John Squire had written a preface, he could claim to be a fellow author. Reginald skimmed through the book one afternoon at the British Museum, at which he spent a good deal of time doing research for his own books, and later Stanley lent us a copy; he was very anxious for us to read it, and Reginald had every intention of reading it properly, but somehow he never did—perhaps because he had already decided when he had run through it at the B.M. that it was really not very good. It was autobiographical, and concerned a holiday he had spent with a young man—Stanley was homosexual. He was also epileptic, so that his problems could be said to be physio-psychological. His homosexuality extended in a sense to his 'jobs', for he never took women's clothes, and whilst awaiting trial he had been quite shocked when it was suggested that a dress I had mislaid in the general confusion of clearing-up and sorting-out after the burglary had been included in his loot. A detective assured Reginald that Stanley was 'quite positive he had not taken it'; he had said he hadn't, and the police had always found Stanley truthful, as well as co-operative. I eventually found the dress, and in fact he took none of my clothes.

I have forgotten, now, how Stanley landed a job in Rye, in Sussex, soon after he came out of Parkhurst, but I went to Hastings to see him; he met me at the station and took me to meet the very nice probation officer who was keeping a friendly eye on him whilst he was in the district. After that we went to Rye by 'bus, and he took me to his employers' flat

—they were away—in which he also had a room. It was a flashy, de luxe apartment, and I mistrusted the job, from what Stanley told me of his employers, and from the vulgarity of the flat itself, and I had an uneasy feeling that it wouldn't last—that it was all too good to be true, too essentially the 'piece of cake' Stanley said it was, and that there must be a catch in it. My misgivings proved true, and it was not long before Stanley was writing me from Wandsworth prison, having come a cropper again. It seemed that the job at Rye had 'packed up' and he had come to London, always a dangerous place for him, and it was part of Stanley's psychological problem that in a crisis such as being out of a job he would never go to the Labour Exchange or Social Security to seek help, but always resorted to burglary, and when the Rye job packed up he had repeated his pattern and had apparently been caught redhanded this time. He was, he wrote me, very much ashamed, but he hoped I would forgive him, and he would be grateful if I would put in an application for a visit and come and see him. . . .

I did, of course, telling myself that Reginald would have done so, and had one of those visits in which one sits in an open booth and talks to the prisoner through a kind of railway station booking-office window, which is not only inhibiting but makes for difficulty of hearing. There is a long row of these booths, and on a stool in each sits a visitor trying to converse through the small window, whilst a warder promenades up and down. Anyhow, we had a conversation of sorts, and I promised Stanley I would speak for him when he 'came up' at the Guildhall, at the Middlesex Assizes, and asked what I could do for him meantime. Well, he said, books and papers, of course—posh Sundays, and the literary mags such as I'd sent him to Parkhurst; and he could have fruit and chocolate. I said I'd see to that, and he thanked me, then asked if I would do him a favour. I said I would if I could.

He then asked me if I would collect some laundry he had left in Fulham; it was good stuff, he said, silk shirts and pyjamas he had got at a job he'd done, and he wouldn't like to lose them.

I was affronted by the request, though, to be sure, it was a measure of his trust in me. I said I couldn't possibly go and collect his stolen goods.

'You should tell the police where they are so that they can be given back to their lawful owner!' I said, sternly.

'Tell the cops?' he exclaimed. 'No fear! They'd collect the stuff all right—and stick to it!'

It was to his credit, I suppose, that he didn't hold it against me that I wouldn't do him the favour. But I did try to send him the fruit and chocolate he had said he could have, and I bought some cakes as well, and trekked back to the prison with it all—only to be told that it wasn't permitted to send in food— 'Only on a plate—a proper meal.'

I protested that I didn't live in the district and I hadn't a car and it would be too difficult to bring a Proper Meal all the way from Wimbledon; would it do, I suggested, if I went and bought a plate and put everything on to it?

'That's not a proper meal,' the copper, not unreasonably, pointed out.

In retrospect I don't know, really, why I so stubbornly felt I must produce that Proper Meal, on a plate; perhaps it was because I had disappointed Stanley over his request about the laundry and had said I would do something about the fruit and chocolate. Anyhow, I went away and bought a plate, then went into a delicatessen and bought slices of cooked meat, and some potato salad and other oddments, and I arranged them on the plate, and covered the plate with a piece of grease-proof paper provided by the delicatessen, then trekked back to the prison. I was readmitted and carried the plate across the wide open space of the yard to the office where permitted articles for prisoners could be handed in. I unveiled the plate and revealed the meat, with the potatoes sitting snugly beside it.

'A proper meal,' I said, firmly.

The copper gave it the once-over and accepted it for the prisoner, Frank A. Stanley.

It was a small victory, but I never repeated the performance. Instead I wrote a piece about it for the then *Manchester Guardian,* which was duly reprinted in a Prison Officers' magazine—from which someone wrote to me, saying they had all been amused.

I did not visit Stanley again before he came up at the Middlesex Assizes, and the next time I saw him was at the Guildhall. I had sent a letter to the court beforehand, asking to be allowed to speak on behalf of Frank A. Stanley, and giving some indication of my long association with him. I was received very courteously by the bench, and the Chairman said, 'I take it you consider there is some good in Stanley?'

'I think there is a great deal of good,' I said, and cited by way of example how distressed he had been when I had told him that he had stolen my late husband's treasured Irish tweed suit, his only good suit, a gift from me, and made from a length of handwoven tweed I had brought back from Connemara, and how when Stanley's mother had died, whilst he was in Parkhurst, serving his seven years P.D., and he had inherited a little money he had obtained permission from the Governor of the prison to send my husband £10 towards replacing the suit, and how I had in fact spent the money on another length of tweed, and another suit had been made, and my husband had worn it when we had gone to visit Stanley in Parkhurst, and how when my husband had died in 1958 I had this suit, which he had always called his burglar suit, made into a suit for me, and this suit I was now wearing. . . .

It was a good story, enough to melt the heart of any bench of justices, and it had the virtue of being absolutely true. The bench adjourned, and when they came back they had decided not to send Stanley to prison again—I had already reminded them that he had recently served seven years P.D. and it had obviously not done him any good—but put him on three years' probation.

I thanked the bench, and Stanley and I left the court together. He kept saying how he could never thank me enough, and on this surge of gratitude we came out into the sunny open spaces of Westminster, with Parliament Square across the road. As we walked in the direction of a 'bus stop Stanley asked me how I liked his overcoat. I had observed that he had been wearing an expensive-looking coat, obviously good material and well-tailored, though a bit on the big side for him. I said, what was true, that it was a very nice coat.

He plucked affectionately at a sleeve.

'Good cloth,' he said, 'and the coat's good as new!' He added, proudly, 'I got it on a job I did.'

I don't remember now what I said in reply. Nothing, probably. Perhaps I said, 'You're the limit!'

I hope I didn't; it would have been natural, but too obvious.

But he was never in trouble with the police again after that. He went to live in a hostel for discharged prisoners, many of them 'old lags' such as himself, and I went to see him there, and had lunch with him and various of the others; he had a good room, and the atmosphere was friendly; everyone accepted everyone else, and no one asked questions. There was a very nice woman who was a kind of house-mother to them all, and who eventually married one of the inmates. Stanley got a job as road-sweeper, which he didn't mind, and then as night-watchman in a block of flats, and eventually as porter in a Fulham hospital. He then left the hostel, which was in north London, and had a one-room furnished flat in the area, and there I went to tea with him. He had bought a great pile of thick white ham sandwiches and some garish cakes for the occasion. The flat was in a respectable old-fashioned house in a quiet, suburban road lined by such houses, with privet hedges and trees. Stanley was very proud of the flat and he had written me that he was 'longing to show it off'. We sat by the gas-fire and I did my best with the thick sandwiches and the garish cakes, and the strong Indian tea, and Stanley talked about his job at the hospital, which he enjoyed doing, and finally opened the door at the bottom of a side-board and commanded me to 'Look at that!'

What I looked at was packets of tea and sugar and tins of evaporated milk, packets and packets and tins and tins. I asked him why he bought such quantities of these things— enough to set up a grocery shop, I declared.

'I don't buy them,' he said. 'I get them at the hospital.'

'You mean you pinch them?'

He grinned.

'They don't miss them.'

I was really exasperated, then.

Author with her burglar, Frank Stanley wearing his 'best suit', at Norman House 1962, after his release from Parkhurst Prison

Reginald Reynolds wearing his 'burglar suit', the money for which was sent him by Stanley, from Parkhurst, to replace the one stolen from him

Sammy, the 'little feller'

Oak Cottage, to which the author came in the summer of 1929 and where she still lives

'You're a fool,' I told him, angrily. 'You with your record! If you were caught you'd be inside again!'

'It's all right,' he assured me, and closed the cupboard door, no doubt disappointed in me.

I never saw him again, though he continued to write.

Then there was the letter in which he wrote that he had a lump in his shoulder and was going into the Marsden, the cancer hospital, for an operation, and he was very worried. 'Wish me luck,' he wrote.

I wrote wishing him luck, and pointing out that not every lump is necessarily malignant, but that even if his should prove to be there was no reason why he shouldn't make a good recovery.

I never had a reply to that letter. I would have gone to see him if he had written to me saying he would like me to. I learned later that he died there and was buried in South London. He would have been sixty-something.

Poor Mr. Stanley.

Some of the story is amusing in its preposterousness, but I think all the same it is one of the sadder stories of my life.

2

Young Man in a Parma Violet Shirt

It was the five o'clock train from Leeds to London; the business man's train, just as the 7.55 from King's Cross in the morning is, and you see the same executives on it. The 7.55 gets you to Leeds by ten-thirty, which means you can be at a board meeting,, or whatever, by eleven, with a good two hours clear before a luncheon appointment at one, with plenty of time after even a protracted lunch before you need head back for the City Station and the five o'clock to King's Cross, at which it arrives soon after seven-thirty.

I was on that train on my way back from Haworth, where I had been looking into the Brontë industry for a chapter in the book I was writing, *England my Adventure*.* London–Haworth and back in a day is no mean trip, let me tell you. I had left the house at six-thirty that morning and reached home at nine in the evening, which adds up to a pretty long day. To reach Haworth from London by train you travel to Leeds, and from there by another line to Keighley; at Keighley you traverse the long, uphill high street to the 'bus station, and there you flounder around until you find a 'bus for Haworth. This sets you down near the Worth Valley station (with its toy trains that go puff-puff off to Oxenhope), and then all you have to do is to toil up the very steep

* 1972.

main street to the parsonage. Well, I did all that, but I did not
like it very much at Haworth, being somewhat allergic to the
Brontë cult, and when I found that if I got a move on I could
catch a 'bus from Keighley to Leeds that would make it possible to get the five o'clock back to London I got that move
on. I reached Leeds with some time in hand and had a look
around and found it no mean city, yet what bliss it was to board
the five o'clock train! I looked forward to the good high tea
such as I had enjoyed on other trains returning from the
North, but the five o'clock back from Leeds does not do high
tea but early dinner, and instead of cosy teaposts and toasted
scones in the first-class dining-car there were gins-and-tonics
and vodkas-on-the-rocks and a smell of cooking. I contented
myself with a stout, telling myself that when you're a bit hun-
gry as well as tired there's nothing like it, and feeling as little
like dinner on the train at 6 p.m. as I'd felt like egg-and-bacon
breakfast at 8 a.m.

I sat opposite a severe looking gentleman who ordered gin-
and-tonic and dinner, and who was as little disposed to talk
to me as I was to him. He sipped his gin-and-tonic and looked
at a local evening paper, and I sipped my stout and looked
around the coach, in which I was apparently the only
female, and then I saw the astonishing young man in the
parma violet shirt.

He was astonishing because he was incredibly handsome
and different. What on earth was he doing amongst all those
business executives, paunchy and middle-aged for the most
part, short-back-and-sides, brief cases, dark lounge suits, the
lot? This young man with his thick, dark longish hair, his dark-
skinned Latin good looks, his splendid parma violet silk shirt
freely displayed across his broad shoulders, his jacket above
him in the rack; this young man with the Ivor Novello profile
and high forehead and sensitive intelligent face, totally
absorbed in a book.

Never have I seen anyone so totally absorbed in a book. He
sipped his gin-and-tonic, and later his soup, without ever
taking his eyes from the page. All through the fish and entrée,
the sweet and the cheese, and the coffee, he had the book in
his lap, and the food on his plate received the bare minimum

of attention, though, quite dexterously, it was forked and cut up and found its way to his mouth. He called for the check and paid it in the same book-bound trance, and when the table was cleared he leaned back in his corner reading—reading . . .

It was a big book, a fat book, and I wondered, inevitably, always interested in what people are reading, always curious to see titles, whether it was fiction or non-fiction; some fascinating biography, perhaps, or absorbing memoirs. Whatever it was it did not raise even the faintest smile. He had good lips, finely modelled, but not sensual; the mouth was firm—even a little hard, I thought. I wondered about his nationality; Spanish? Italian? Even Greek, perhaps. Definitely European, and racially Aryan. Not English, I thought; at most only half English.

I wondered what he had to do with Leeds; there was a repertory theatre, so perhaps he was an actor; there was a university, so perhaps he taught. On the other hand, of course, he might simply be in the 'rag trade', since he had boarded the train at Leeds. Perhaps some of the younger men in the trade looked like that nowadays, despite the preponderance of the conventional executive type all round. Perhaps he was the young man in the Leeds rag trade who was different.

But different he certainly was; not since General Abdel Karim Qassim of Iraq had I seen a man possessed of so much *charisma*. He wore no wedding ring and I wondered if he was married, or had a mistress; he did not suggest homosexuality. But he did not suggest an ardent heterosexuality either; there was something a little cold, even, about that handsome face.

I had two hours and forty minutes in which to study him and speculate about him, and since he never once looked up from his book I could do it as unremittingly as he read. His presence in that compartment full of business executive types was like a gift; a blessing. The face of a beautiful girl or woman in a crowd, the handsome face of a man—striking, intelligent, interesting—such faces, which are so very rare, are always that—a gift, a blessing, life coming up to beg one's pardon for all the ugliness, physical and spiritual, and make this offering of the sweet and lovely face of a woman, the good looks of a man.

Was this handsome young man 'good'—that is to say kind, generous-hearted, unselfish, concerned for the sufferings of his fellow-man, capable of love in the real sense—the 'ability to give and the willingness to suffer', as Maude Royden nobly defined it* years ago? 'Good looks', we say, meaning only pul-chritude, physical attractiveness, but the good looks are not necessarily good except on that aesthetic level; yet purely on that level they are a gift and a blessing. I finished my stout and signalled the waiter for another. What, in *hell*, was the book the young man found so totally engrossing?

We came into King's Cross dead on time. The young man abruptly closed his book, stuffed it into a brief case, stood up and took down from the rack his jacket and a small suitcase. Before he stuffed the book away I strained forward and read the title. It conveyed nothing at all; it could equally have been a novel or a biography. Yet at the back of my mind I had an idea I had read something—inveterate review-reader that I am—about a book of that title.

The young man shrugged himself into his jacket, and I found satisfaction in the fact that he was tall, as well as broad-shouldered, and that his movements were easy, graceful—well, they should be; he could not have been more than about thirty-two, and he could have been less. There was a curious kind of anguish in the thought that in a few minutes, when we all left the train, he would stride away across the station and I would never see him again.

I had a fantasy in which I approached him on the platform : 'Will you forgive a complete stranger, but I was so interested in your absorption in the book you were reading on the train —as a writer myself . . .' and I would perhaps give him my card; he would tell me the title of the book, and I would say yes, I had noticed the title, but was it a novel—a biography— or what? And who was the author? He would smile then— and I longed to see him smile, for a smile is a light; it illuminates—and tell me about the book, and we could chat a little, and this would enable me to ask him his profession, even his nationality—or origins. This encounter would be only a matter of a few minutes, but at the end of it I would know

* In *The Threefold Cord,* 1947.

about him. I would thank him, apologise again for intruding on him, and we would part, pleasantly. I still would never see him again, but it would not matter. No more would have been called for. Curiosity would have been satisfied. But to have him just walk away like that, with the book, the clue to his personality, unidentified—that, exaggerated as the statement sounds, was a kind of anguish.

But he left the train and strode away, and I did not accost him, and I crossed the dreary concourse of King's Cross and went down into the tube, and I felt stricken; you could almost say bereaved.

There are people who enter into one's imagination. They are very few, but when they do the impact is profound. No one has ever made the impact on me that Qassim of Iraq did, in 1962. I am very well aware of his shortcomings as Head of State, but he was neither mad nor bad, as his detractors asserted; and as a human being he had more in the way of *charisma* than any one person has a right to—as I wrote in *A Lance for the Arabs.**

The impact of his personality was the impact of tremendous personal charm plus good looks. And that *je ne sais quoi* of physique, of narrow hips, of animal grace of movement. For me, too, all that made him unsatisfactory as a statesman—his introversion, megalomania, sense of Messianic mission—made him interesting.

The young man on the train was probably of no real interest at all; the Ivor Novello profile and the thick, waving dark hair might be attributable to Italian parentage. He was probably a London-born Italian in the Leeds rag trade, but being young, and not guaranteed English-made, was just that much different from his middle-aged British-business-man colleagues, so that whereas they sat there in the first-class dining-car correct in their well-tailored dark suitings and reading the evening papers, he sat there jacketless in his beautiful parma violet silk shirt and read—unremittingly—that book. That book which I was so sure was the key to his personality.

I would never see him again; I would never know his profession, his nationality, or anything about him—but if I could

* 1962.

know something about that book I would have at least a clue.

I could not consult my old librarian friend, Gilbert Turner, because he was in hospital undergoing surgery, but his deputy was co-operative. I could only give him the title of the book; could not tell him whether it was fiction or non-fiction, or the author's name; only the title, and that it was a big fat book. He produced various books, both fiction and non-fiction, of similar titles. But a title is a title, and if a book is called *the* something it is no use producing a book called just something. Also, I repeated, it was a *fat* book. . . .

In the end he produced it. I unpacked it, and there it was, just as I had seen it on the train when the young man had finally closed it and laid it on the table before stuffing it into his brief case, when I had seen its title so clearly, unmistakably. I opened it, eagerly, skimmed down the blurb on the inside flap of the jacket, and was a little disappointed to discover that it was a novel. An American novel. I began to read, to review-read, rapidly; and within the first few pages was pulled up short by a passage of what was to me a quite startling degree of pornography. I skimmed on for a bit, but it seemed only an interminable series of the most explicitly detailed sexual episodes. I sent it back by return of post, telling myself bleakly, that, well, anyhow now I knew.

3

Race Relations

This is another story of a train journey back to London from the North, and I was again travelling first-class because I had again been given a pass by British Rail for what I had to do there. I entered the train this time at Wigan, after my third and last visit to that very pleasant town, in June, 1972.

There was only one occupant of the non-smoker I entered, a young black girl seated in a corner by the window. She was somewhat hippy of appearance, with various dilapidated carrier bags disposed at her feet, and a shabby suitcase in the rack above her. But nowadays there is no reason to assume that because someone is young, black, and a bit scruffy that person has no legal right in a first-class compartment of British Rail. I was only mildly surprised—and interested.

When I entered she looked up from a magazine in her lap; I smiled and observed that it was cold.

'It's freezing!' she declared, and sprang up and closed the window and turned on the heating in both corners. I wondered, vaguely, settling myself into a corner by the door, why she hadn't done all that earlier if she was that cold.

I took a book out of my handbag and tried to read, but it soon became fearfully hot in the compartment, making concentration difficult. I hoped she would herself become aware of the heat and airlessness and turn off one of the heaters and open the window a crack, but did not care to suggest it, telling myself that perhaps she was not yet acclimatised to the rigors of the English summer and *needed* all that heat, and that with any luck she wasn't going all the way to London; but she appeared to be oblivious of the furnace conditions she had created and went on with her magazine; I tried to read but soon dozed off, overcome.

I was wakened by the sliding of the compartment door and a peremptory, 'Tickets, please!'

I showed my immaculate white ticket, which was clipped and collected. The inspector then reached across for the slip of paper the black girl fished out of her shabby handbag. Examining it he was immediately infuriated.

'Second-class!' he shouted. 'This is a first-class compartment! Can't you read?'

He pointed to FIRST plainly marked on the window by which she sat.

'I was bought the ticket,' she said, as though that explained everything. She played it cool, as though it was nothing whatever to do with her. Her manner only very mildly protested.

But that inspector he played it very far from cool. He played it hot as the compartment itself.

'You was bought a *second-class* ticket,' he roared at her, and repeated, 'You was bought a second-class ticket and you are in a *first-class* compartment! So you owe me some money, see?'

Curious wording, I thought. If she owed anyone any money it wasn't this bullying inspector but the British Railways Board, and since they had recently coughed up two millions sterling in wage claims did it really matter?

'I haven't any money,' the black girl stated, sullenly, still playing it cool.

For a moment the inspector seemed non-plussed, then he said, violently, 'You haven't any money! O.K. I'll let you off this time, but get out! *Get out!* Next time you'll end up in a police court, see? Now *get out!*'

The girl got up, unhurriedly, collected her carrier bags and dumped them on the seat, dragged her shabby suitcase down from the rack.

'Where shall I go?' she demanded, in that same cool tone, half sullen, half indifferent. It added up, perhaps, to a kind of insolence. Admirable, in a way. Anyone standing up to bullying is admirable, even if in the wrong.

'Go where you like!' he bawled at her. 'Back down the corridor! Anywhere that isn't marked *first*!'

Then, astonishingly, in what seemed a climax of fury, he added, 'And don't pull your colour on *me*!'

I wish, now, I had asked him what he meant by that, for she wasn't pulling anything on anyone; she did not reply, but merely bundled out of the compartment and headed down the corridor to the crowded second-class.

To me this abominable man observed, angrily, 'I can't always be checking these second-class!' Then added his second *non-sequitur*, 'You can't win!'

Alone in the compartment I turned off the heat and opened the window.

I should have intervened, I thought miserably. I should have protested, 'There's no need to shout at her! Perhaps she doesn't understand the British railways system of first and second class!'

Why hadn't I come to her defence? I don't reckon to be a person lacking in moral courage. I didn't really know; nor do I now. I can only think that by such a sudden, short and sharp, assault and battery of verbal attack, one is stunned.

I wondered, too, whether that inspector would have behaved like that, as aggressively, as offensively, if the offender had been white. If he had he would perhaps have got his answer. But then the offender would not have been 'let off', I suspect, but booked for prosecution. It was something that the bully had at least let the black girl off. But what on earth had he meant by telling her not to pull her colour on him? She had made no protest about being bullied because she was black; indeed, she had made no protest at all, but merely, keeping her cool, offhandedly asked where she should go. Had there been some complicated upsurge of conscience on the inspector's part, involving his decision to let her off this time?

I should have asked him. I should not have allowed him to slide the door on the whole episode. *Mea culpa!* It was bad race relations all round. Whether that black girl was transgressing from negligence, stupidity, or in the hope of getting away with it, or simply from non-comprehension of the class system on British railways, she is no doubt now going around telling people how she was turned out of a first-class compartment because she was black, and, worse still, she probably believes it. She probably was just chancing it, hoping to get away with it, and was lucky to have done so. It isn't really the point. The point is that her transgression produced a quite disproportionate rage in the inspector.

It would be merely a train incident, rather than a story, but for the fact that as soon as the inspector had gone on down the corridor a white boy and girl, hippie-style, trendily scruffy, strung with haversacks and guitars, moved triumphantly and hilariously into the first-class compartment next door. . . .

As my daughter likes to say, the only point of this story is that it's true.

4

Long Day's Journey into Windsor

That goes for this story, too; and, again, the sting is in the tail of the tale.

My old friend, Tim Ziemsen, and I had thought to combine a visit to a mutual friend, another old friend, the distinguished Borough Librarian, Gilbert Turner, who had gone to live in Windsor, with a picnic in the park. We planned to arrive in Windsor around noon, make our way up to the park, eat our sandwiches, do a good walk, and arrive at Gilbert's for tea, around four, a plan which seemed to all concerned most admirable.

Had Tim and I simply met at Paddington to entrain for Windsor all would have been well, but, said I, why go all the way into town when we can meet at Putney and take a train to Twickenham, with a saving of time, energy, and fares? He agreed that it was a good idea, and we each did a short 'bus ride to Putney and met there mid-morning, in nice time to reach Windsor by mid-day. It was a sunny September day, ideal for a picnic and walk in the park.

At Twickenham we felt ourselves in luck, for a sign board indicated the train for Windsor as the next train. We boarded the train very cheerfully, congratulating ourselves on our luck, and on it being such a lovely day for the outing. I chatted away about how in my youth I had lived at Strawberry Hill, near Twickenham, and how well I knew this neighbourhood. Tim, who remains something of a foreigner despite

British naturalisation and many years in the country, politely regarded the scene from the window and agreed that it was a very pleasant neighbourhood, and the neighbours of this hood —no doubt they also were pleasant?

I did not bother to explain about neighbourhoods and neighbours because I was already a little puzzled. Uneasy, even. I had not expected Hounslow. I lapsed into an anxious silence, broken at Isleworth by a declaration of my unease.

'I don't understand,' I said, 'how we reach Windsor by this route.'

'On the indicator at Twickenham,' Tim said, reassuringly, 'I do not remember seeing Isleworth, but certainly I saw Staines and Windsor. Perhaps it was not important to mention Isleworth. It does not look to be much of a hood!'

I offered no comment, but when we reached Chiswick I exclaimed, 'This is impossible! We are heading back for Putney!'

Tim, who is of a sanguine disposition, which he likes to attribute to being Continental, laughed.

'That would be *très drôle*!'

He gazed happily out of the window.

'Certainly it is not an attractive hood, but it is an adventure, is it not?'

'It is nothing of the kind!' I snapped. 'It is a damned waste of time! Whatever that indicator at Twickenham said this train isn't going to Staines and Windsor. It is going to Kew and Putney!'

'Then from Putney we will take again the train to Twickenham,' declared my murderee of a friend, adding, cheerfully, 'The day is still young!'

Then, realising that I was a very long way from finding the situation droll, but was, on the contrary, irritated and exasperated, urged that we should be philosophical. We should, after all, reach Windsor eventually, and not too late.

'Not too late for tea, anyhow!' I said bitterly.

We got back to Putney just an hour after I had set out. From Wimbledon, where I live, Putney is a ten minutes' 'bus ride.

With a wait at Putney for a train back to Twickenham, and an even longer wait at Twickenham for the Windsor train, we reached Windsor exactly three hours after our first arrival at Putney.

Tim remained imperturbably cheerful, continuing to find it amusing. He agreed that it was tiresome that the wrong indicator should have been put up at Twickenham, or, more likely, that the indicator for the previous train had not been taken down.

'You will write to the station master and complain,' said he. 'You will write also to the Chief Public Relations Officer of the British Railways Board.'

I said grimly that I would do that all right, but that it wouldn't give us back our lost hour. The P.R.O. would reply politely regretting the negligence (and this, in fact, he duly did) but by that time the incident would have become merely one of life's innumerable minor irritations; meantime there was the consuming sense of frustration. Three hours to Windsor! I had not suffered from such a sense of impotent rage since a woman customs official on Moscow airport emptied the entire contents of my suitcase out on the counter and left me to put it all back.

Well, anyhow, I thought, when we stepped out on to the platform at Windsor riverside station at last, we can go and have a well-earned drink in the station buffet—a nourishing stout and one would feel better; undoubtedly.

We entered the buffet and Tim went up to the counter and ordered the drinks, and I seated myself at a table.

The girl behind the bar said something; Tim looked puzzled and repeated the order thinking she had not understood. She repeated what she had said and he came over to me.

'I think we cannot be served,' he said. 'Perhaps you had better speak with her.'

'Can't be served? Why ever not? It's not out-of-hours and we're both over eighteen!'

I got up and went over to the bar.

'My friend doesn't understand,' I said. 'We would like two stouts, please.'

She said, 'I've told the gentleman. I can't serve you. Only with soft drinks.'

'But why?' I demanded. 'The buffet is licensed to sell beer and spirits, and it's not out-of-hours. *Why* can't you serve us?'

Then, astonishingly, she said, tossing her head, *'I'm not old enough!'*

She was young, it is true, but I'd not have thought as young as all that. One of those who mature early, evidently.

I said, 'Then what are you doing in this bar?'

'Minding it for my aunt,' she said.

This time is was I who wanted to laugh; but hysterically. Mercifully there was a pub just round the corner—where the bartender was fully old enough to serve us.

As I was saying, the only point of this story is that it is true.

5

At the Concert

It is a shockingly uncultural admission, I know well, but whilst I would find life very difficult to sustain without books I could get along quite well without music. I cannot, really, imagine a life without books, but a life in which there was no music would not trouble me at all, for, in fact, I very seldom listen to music. I like the music of Johann Sebastian Bach very much, especially the Brandenburg Concerto No. 5, the slow movement of the Concerto for Two Violins, and the whole of the St. Matthew Passion. In desert-island-discs terms, if I could have only one composer it would have to be Bach. I have never heard anything by him that has not given me pleasure. I have a good many Bach records; but I almost never play them. I like Beethoven's A Minor Quartet; and odds and ends of Mozart and Purcell. In the twenties and early thirties, when I was a balletomane, I was mad about Ravel and Debussy. I like some of Wagner's Ring music very much, though I cannot bear *Tristan and Isolde*. In general I dislike opera quite intensely. I knew a man once who when he went to the ballet shut his eyes so that he would not see the antics on the stage but only hear the music. I feel the same way about opera. If there was to be the music of only one composer in the world I would settle for Bach. But I can get along quite well without even that strong clear voice. Whereas I would find it very hard indeed to get along without books.

G. K. Chesterton is reputed to have replied, when asked if he liked music, that he 'didn't mind it'. I do mind it; I like only

General Abdel Karim Qassim, Prime Minister of Iraq, shot by the Ba'athists in the *coup* of February 8, 1963

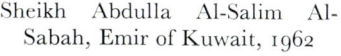

Khalid Zaki, Iraqi revolutionary, killed in armed conflict with the police and military in the marshes near Basra, May 1968

Sheikh Abdulla Al-Salim Al-Sabah, Emir of Kuwait, 1962

'Tim' (F. W. Ziemsen) at Oak Cottage

Oak Cottage; looking down from the little wood at the top of the slope
above the loggia, at the side of the house

a very little of it, and that I do not want to hear often. Occasionally I have gone to concerts; not of my own volition, but because I have been invited, and the programme being 'my kind of music' I have accepted . . . which I never should have, for I have invariably dozed off during the slow movements. But now I have been to my last concert. The friend whose guest I was at that one, being of a tolerant disposition, was good enough to invite me to the 1972 Prom concert at which all the Brandenburg concertos were done in the one evening —something very rare. I love the Brandenburg concertos, and especially number five, but I did not accept; instead I wrote this good friend that it would be no good—'I would only get the wee-wees, the coughs, the dozings-off.' All of which overtook me at that last concert, which was also a Bach occasion.

The story begins with the gin-and-tonic in the bar before the concert began, and which proved to be a mistake, for it quickly reached the bladder; but how was one to know? I decided to slip out at the end of the first movement, and to sit at the back, not attempt to return to my place, for the second movement. I murmured to my friend that I was 'just going to the loo', and made my way to the exit, in that minute or so between movements. It was at the Festival Hall, and quite a long march to the Ladies, but I was not worried, confident that I need not disturb anyone on my return.

I reached my objective and was just leaving when a member of the St. John Ambulance first-aid corps hurried up to me, demanding, anxiously, 'Are you all right? The gentleman said you were feeling faint.'

'Me?' I asked, puzzled. 'Not me. I'm feeling fine, thanks. I just popped out to the loo.'

It was her turn to look puzzled.

'You aren't the lady who was feeling faint? The gentleman said the lady in the red dress.'

I was wearing a red dress and felt quite apologetic about it. 'Sorry,' I said, smiling. 'I'm not that lady.'

I left her and marched on across the huge foyer, and then saw my friend hurrying towards me.

'Are you all right?' he demanded, anxiously, as he came

L

up with me. 'I was worried, and the first-aid lady said she'd go along and see if you were all right—I thought you said you were feeling faint . . .'

'I'm terribly sorry,' I said. 'I told you I was going to the loo.'

'Oh, what a relief!'

'Yes,' I said, 'it was.'

We slipped in through the swing doors and into seats at the end of the row, without disturbing anyone. A slow movement was being played—very beautiful, very quiet; I listened intently, and then began to be aware of a tickle at the back of my throat. It would be too awful to cough when the house was so hushed, the music so soft. I tightened the muscles of my throat. Mind over matter. I held my breath until I could hold it no longer. The tickle persisted. A tiny choke escaped me once, and I made another superhuman effort. I thought the movement would never end. When at last it did I allowed the cough to explode in the minute or so before the final movement began.

I did not cough again after that, nor have the slightest desire to. I relaxed and enjoyed the music, the lovely rise and fall of the strings, the soft sweet singing of the solo violin . . . and woke with a start as the applause broke out at the end.

My friend was very nice about it; he agreed that *andante* movements could be soporific, and I, of course, made my usual joke about being able to sleep almost anywhere except in a bed. It was gallant of him to take another chance with me and invite me to the Bach Promenade Concert the following year, but I am sure I was right to decline. I am safer at home with the record-player on the rare occasions when I am in the mood to let the sound of music creep in my ears.

I don't know, really, why people do go to concerts, to sit in rows looking at the backs of necks, when every kind of music is available through the media of television and radio to a high degree of perfection, live or through high-fidelity recordings. Music, surely, is something to be enjoyed in the comfort and privacy of one's own home, or in the home of a good friend, not sitting on upright chairs in rows, in a public place, and surrounded by a crowd of strangers. I have never really understood it; but then I am not 'musical'.

6

The Little Feller

(For cat people only)

In January, 1967, a three-year-old ginger tom-cat became very much a story in my life, and nearly six years later, as I write this it is a continuing story. In the first few months it was hard-going for both of us, for an uprooted, bewildered, frightened cat can be as maladjusted to new conditions and environment as a pushed-around child, and react as aggressively. The story of the cat's rehabilitation I told, quite unsentimentally, in a little book I called *My Cat Sammy*,* though the title I wanted was *The Little Feller* and I still prefer it, but the publishers disliked it. Here, for anyone interested I want to continue the story a little further, for the little feller is still part of my scene, and a progress-report on him seems in order. Apart from the fact that I like to write it. If I were an artist I would make drawings and paintings of him, but I can only set him down in words.

I like, admire, and respect cats; I find them beautiful and interesting, but I don't think I am a 'cat lover'; I don't go to cat shows, am not in the least interested in breeds, and detest sentimental writings about cats. I dislike, quite intensely, calendars and postcards depicting pretty pussies; I don't like pretty pussies, or pussy people. I just like cats; the common or garden cat, and the commoner the better.

* 1971.

So that for me the entirely proletarian young ginger tom entirely filled the feline bill. None of the sinuous grace of a Siamese—or any of those high-class cats—about him; he is stocky, with short, strong legs and a massive head—'like a little lion', as the young vet who attended him once said. He stumps along on his big pads, and every so often limps, but whether from rheumatism or some injury incurred in the affrays he makes, or becomes involved in, I don't know. I know nothing about his private life, which is nocturnal, the way Nature designed it for the feline species. In Ilford whence he came, he had a sex life, rich and full; I doubt if he has any here, for this is a select residential suburb, and the bourgeoisie are great on emasculation—in all senses, but when it comes to cats it's called neutering. There are a few cats in this primarily dog area, but spayed or castrated, according to sex. The castrated males have still enough aggressiveness in them to give this little feller a thick ear when he invades their territories, but his chances of ever meeting an unspayed female, and in season at that, are, I greatly fear, nil.

How much this irks him I have no idea. It would worry me if I let it. I have been told that the male animal is not subject to the perpetual sexual itch that plagues the human male; that it is only sexually excited by proximity to the female in season. I would like to think this is true, but I wonder. From the little I know of dogs, and my observation of their behaviour, it would not appear to be true of them. I have been assured that it is true of cats. Whether it was wishful thinking on the part of the cat person who told me, who shall say? If external signs are anything to go by—a built-in, almost non-stop purr, a good appetite—whether for raw minced steak or the cheapest kind of tinned cat-food—and an enormous capacity for sleep, then my-cat-Sammy is a contented cat.

He is also, for a cat, remarkably affectionate. At least, I think it is remarkable. I have had cats most of my adult life, but until I acquired this little 'Ilford tiger' I always maintained that, unlike dogs, cats were incapable of affection; but after an initial resistance to the idea I have come to the conclusion that this cat does demonstrate affection. Not the devoted loyalty of a dog; of course not; but some kind of liking, shall we say, demonstrated by pushing his head hard against my face or hands, which he does not do with anyone else, all the time purring loudly. If it's not affection I don't know. Perhaps it's just nice to do.

Although he is a full cat he does not 'spray' around the premises, but leaves his cards elsewhere—for what good it does him. He is a good cat, too, in that he does not go after birds, of which there are a great variety in this wooded garden. He has three times caught and killed and eaten baby squirrels, but never a bird. I have, anxiously, observed him watching, not idly, but with an alert interest, a blackbird hopping about within a few yards of him; on occasion he has got up, his tail lashing with anger, but he has, mercifully, made no advance. The last squirrel he caught he played with for a long time before he killed it. I was tempted to intervene, but I didn't; it was, strictly, none of my business.

'Cats are cruel.' I suppose so. They have their fun at the expense of other creatures. Doesn't Man? When you reflect upon the monstrous cruelty human beings inflict on the animal world, with vivisection and factory-farming, in the name of science on the one hand and profitable food production on the other, have we any right at all to call animals, who have no moral pretensions, cruel? I, anyhow, do not think so.

Between my-cat-Sammy and me there is a kind of rough acceptance, overlaid with a thin veneer of affection, I think. When he is annoyed with me he has no compunction at all about biting the hand that feeds him; just as I, when annoyed with him, have no compunction about lifting him with my foot or picking him up and flinging him. He falls on his feet, looks surprised, then saves face in the cat manner by washing himself, as though nothing had happened. Cats, I think, have a dignity quite lacking in dogs. In my observation dogs are friendly, ingratiating creatures, and vulnerable; a dog will cower; a cat fights back, hissing to its last breath.

Sammy has done nothing sensational since his squirrel the summer before last. There have been no bouts of absence-without-leave since the eight-day absence in May, 1970, at the end of which he returned skeleton-thin, coughing from a chicken-bone lodged in his throat—though I did not know this, nor did the vet, for about three weeks, when he finally brought it up—and with pneumonia. He returns sometimes, in the mornings, a bit scratched about the head and chipped about the ears, and limping, but not the heavily wounded warrior of yesteryear. He is nearly nine years old, as I write this, and it is middle-age, I suppose, for a cat. Perhaps he begins, already, to savour the pleasures of retirement. Or at least of semi-retirement. I would like to think so.

To say only that he is a nice little feller, good-natured, amiable, affectionate, is to take too sentimental a line about him; he is all of that, but also he in his cat self, remote from the human beings who stroke him and open tins and make much of him—when they are not shouting at him to shut up and get the hell out of it, lonely, always seeking and never finding, a wanderer in the night who returns weary and empty in the morning; in his domesticated self contented; in his true cat-self—who knows? Certainly not I. I think we know very little about cats; and that that is why some of us, many of us, and writers particularly, find them interesting; fascinating, even.

I think there is not much communication between a human being and a cat, whereas there is a good deal with a dog. Sammy knows when he is being addressed, and he understands, by an inflexion in the voice, when he is being invited to something or other, and responds, though he would not dream of responding to any kind of command. To the invitation he responds eagerly or leisurely; to the command he merely resumes sleep, pretends not to have heard, or sits up and washes in a marked manner.

In the summer he looks terrible, thin and scrawny after the moult, like a sheep after shearing; in the autumn, when he has grown his winter coat he is, as Dr. Johnson said of his Hodges, 'a very fine cat.' (Though he acknowledged that there were many handsomer.) In the autumn he takes on a kind of protective colouring among the golden leaves or lying in a patch of mellow sunshine.

People say, 'He must be great company for you!' But of course he's not; when he's in the house he's invariably asleep, and at nights, when I sit here working, he's out—doing whatever it is he does do at nights. But that's all right; he lives his life and I live mine, both of us pretty solitary, as is suited to our respective natures, and in the morning we meet and rub heads. He's anyhow a cat of character, the little feller.

Since writing the foregoing some six months ago, in the late autumn of 1972, Sammy has used up the last of his nine lives and is no more. The following April he developed lymphosarcoma, deteriorated rapidly during a ten-day illness, during which time he almost ceased to eat and drink and became from 'a very fine cat' a bag of skin and bones. He was attended by the nice young Scots vet who restored him to health in May, 1970, when he was similarly a skeleton-cat; but this time there was nothing that anti-biotic injections and pills could do for him, for he had, as the vet put it, on his first examination, 'something more sinister' than the suspected enteritis. I said, 'You think he has a tumour?' The vet replied, sombrely, 'I'm afraid so.' I said, resolutely, 'In which case there's nothing for it but to put him down?' He nodded, and said that he would come next day and take a blood test. When he came, after taking Sammy's temperature, he said, thoughtfully, that he would like to take him back with him to his surgery; he could take the blood test better there, he said, and also an X-ray. He had a box in the boot of his car. . . . 'And if you don't find anything you'll bring him back this evening?' I ventured to hope. Yes, he said, and echoed my hope. He looked grave.

So for the second time I put a cat into a veterinary box, though after Lucy in 1967 I had vowed never again. I had expected Sammy to protest, but he did not utter, nor when he was carried away down the garden path—though six-and-a-half years ago, when he had been similarly carried up that path, to his new home, he had yelled his head off. Later that afternoon I had the telephone call confirming that the X-ray had revealed a tumour in the abdomen; that it was lymphosarcoma; cancer. No blood test was taken; it was not necessary. He was put down immediately after the phone-call—and my assent. The vet a few days later offered me what comfort he could. 'We didn't keep him hanging about,' he said. I was grateful for that.

It was only a fortnight ago, as I write this, that bright, sunny April afternoon that was the end of the road for My-cat-Sammy, the end of The Saga of Sammy-cat. I still see him everywhere, in the house and garden. It will pass in time, of course, and I'll get used to him being no longer around; but it takes time, and that time is not yet.

He was such a very *nice* little feller. . . .

7

Uninvited Guest

It is my custom never to answer a knock on the front door unless I am expecting someone; even so I have been caught occasionally. The story I am about to relate is not an example of this, however, for that April afternoon in 1969 when a knock came at the door though I was not expecting anyone, nevertheless I answered. I was in the kitchen cutting sandwiches for tea when the knock came; Tim was there, and we had just installed a new electric fire in the sitting-room and looked forward to trying it out over tea. When the knock came my friend came to the kitchen door.

'Don't go,' he urged. 'Or would you like me to, and say you're not here?'

Recklessly I said, 'I'll go. There are those books I'm expecting. There was no post this morning, so perhaps there's a delivery now.'

I went out into the little hall and opened the front door.

A tallish man wearing dark glasses and a brown suède jacket with a sheepskin collar leaned against the wall of the porch. He did not straighten up when I opened the front door, but drawled, 'Hullo, Ethel!'

Not recognising him I stared at him and said, 'I'm sorry . . .'

With a dramatic flourish he whipped off the dark glasses, smiling faintly. The face was rather heavy, middle-aged, the smile vaguely unpleasant. I continued to stare, without recognition, and said again, apologetically, 'I'm sorry . . .'

He then said his name.

It was the name of a man I had known in the Far East fifteen years ago; an Englishman of whose friendship I had been glad at that time; we had made some journeys together, and the affection between us had been real, though, to be sure, we had a few bickers, for he was never less than conceited and arrogant. Had I met him in different circumstances I might have disliked him quite intensely, but at that time, alone, and in a very foreign country, a fellow countryman who took an interest and extended friendship was precious. We had corresponded for a year or two when I got back, but we increasingly irritated each other and the friendship finally lapsed. Then, early in 1966, I was restlessly toying with the idea of making another journey to the Far East; I had had a correspondence with a fan in a Far Eastern country I had never visited; she urged its beauties and interest upon me, and, in the Oriental manner, hospitality. Interest stirred in me; it would be something new, and it would make a book. Also X was living there now, and perhaps after this lapse of years it would be possible to meet again without acrimony? I wrote to him, telling him of my tentative idea, and asked whether, if I carried it out, he would like to see me again, adding that for my part I liked the idea. His reply was devious, to say the least. If I thought I could *bear* to see again anyone I so obviously regarded as a humbug . . . It was a sarcastic and unpleasant letter, and I thought, Well, no, perhaps not, and regretted writing. I would write and say I hadn't been able to raise the cost of the trip, or that my publishers weren't interested in a book about that area, so it wasn't 'on'—it had anyhow been only a tentative idea, as I'd explained. . . .

Then before I had had time to write this letter there came that 5 a.m. telephone call from my old friend, Rickey, from Los Angeles, and I had suddenly realised that the trip I really wanted to make was to California—where I was sure of my welcome. I therefore wrote to X that I wouldn't after all be coming his way as I had decided to visit my old friend in California, and my publishers were interested in a book about an American journey and were not much interested in the idea of another Far Eastern one. All of which was quite true. I went ahead with my plans for the American journey, and in the meantime had an incredibly savage and insulting letter from X accusing me of insulting him by my change of plan, and demanding why didn't I *marry* Rickey whilst I was about it, adding, for whatever it might mean, that it 'would be suitable'.

(At this point I should perhaps say that X was homosexual, so that there was no question of any kind of sex-jealousy such as this fantastic and abusive letter might suggest.)

I did not reply to this letter, and duly sailed for New York. When I was with Rickey in California I had a letter from my daughter in which she said that amongst the mail, which she was looking after in my absence, there was a 'very nasty' post-card from—(she named the country, not the sender; she did not know who was the sender) which she had torn up. She didn't detail the nastiness of the postcard, and I didn't ask her; I could guess at it, and it could only have been from X. I was glad she had torn it up. There was nothing more from him until that Saturday afternoon in April, 1969, when he lounged in the porch and I completely failed to recognise him, forcing him to say his name.

When he said it I was literally stunned. I could not think or speak or feel. I stared at him, and he lounged there against the whitewashed wall, insolently, arrogantly, with that sarcastic smile.

He said, 'Did you think I wouldn't have the audacity?'

Afterwards it seemed to me a strange thing to have said; *audacity,* a somehow dated word; all those years of living in the Far East had put him out of touch; but I'd thought that fifteen years ago when he had believed it *avante garde* to admire T. S. Eliot . . .

I remember that I replied—and that it seemed to come out of some sort of vacuum in myself—'I didn't think anything. I wasn't thinking about you.' That I said it blankly, confusedly, and then mumbled something about 'You'd better come in.'

Instead of taking him into the sitting-room I led him into the kitchen.

'I'm getting tea,' I said, helplessly.

My mind wasn't working. I was, I suppose, in a state of shock.

Tim came in, and I said, perfunctorily, 'This is X,' and to X, 'This is an old and dear friend of mine, Tim Ziemsen.'

Tim, who knew all about X, and his abominable letter on the eve of my departure for America, rose to the occasion admirably, all charm and *savoir faire*. With all the right, polite questions he elicted that X was stopping off in London on his way back from a lecture tour in the U.S.A. I went on cutting bread, spreading butter and paste, making sandwiches, but not with the efficiency with which I had started out; the bread crumbled and I began to cut thick. In a lull in the polite chit-chat I was aware of X's amused watching of the mess I was making of the sandwiches.

'You derange me!' I exclaimed.

'I am sorry to derange you,' he drawled.

Tim went over to the gas cooker, where the kettle was by then boiling its head off, to make tea. I picked up the plate of sandwiches and led the way into the sitting-room, where the table was already laid for tea. Tim brought an extra cup-and-saucer and plate, the teapot and hot water.

X removed his sheepskin jacket and settled himself in an armchair, smiling; endlessly smiling. He had had the audacity; old E was visibly unnerved; her 'boy friend' (which I am sure is how he would have thought of Tim) was working over-time to keep up the social pretences; he, X, who had once boasted to me that he could 'steam-roller anybody in an argument', was in control of the situation. I poured the tea and Tim passed the sandwiches and went gallantly on with the polite conversation.

But X had 'had the audacity' not just to make small talk. He had come to accuse, and he got on with it.

Charge one was that I had put him into my novel, *The Blue-Eyed Boy*. This really startled me. What had X, of the Far East, got to do with this London novel about a delinquent boy? The novel was published in 1959, and ten years later I did not remember it except in broad outline.

'Surely not?' I said.

But oh yes, I did, it seemed; there was a homosexual character from the Far East in the book. 'It was obviously me,' he said, with a kind of gloating satisfaction.

I remembered then that the blue-eyed boy, who had learned that there was money to be got from rich queers if you played along, picked up, at the garage at which he worked, a middle-aged homosexual who had been in the Far East and who liked boys. This man took him for a meal at a Chinese restaurant in the East End—one to which I had myself been taken, and which had reputedly the best Chinese food in London. This homosexual is a very minor character in the novel—merely a passing incident in the boy's life, and not really a character, as such, in the novel at all. Perhaps I had X in mind when I sketched this character in; I really don't know. X was hardly the only Englishman whose pleasure in the life of the Far East was the availability of boys. I knew others. It was typical of X's conceitedness that he should assume that the homosexual in *The Blue-Eyed Boy* was himself.

I said that perhaps I had based this minor character on him; it was all so long ago now, and I didn't remember, and did it really matter? But X waived that point because he had another up his sleeve, good and spiteful. The description of the Chinese meal was idiotic, he declared; 'making the man say "try some of this chop suey"—as though any China Old Hand would mention chop suey! It's unheard of in China!'

I pointed out that the restaurant was in London, and that chop suey features on all menus in the English Chinese restaurants. In this Tim, with whom I have had many meals in Chinese restaurants in London, warmly supported me.

But X was enjoying himself, and was not to be put off by any simple statements of fact. He went on to ask me if I was 'still a vegetarian'. No, I said, not for some years now.

'Curious,' he said, smiling unpleasantly.

He then asked me if I still knew a woman well known in vegetarian and Theosophical circles. He knew that I had known her in the twenties, but by the same token he also knew that our friendship had lapsed in that era. No, I said.

'Curiouser and curiouser,' he observed, complacently.

I made no comment; it was all so stupid, even the Alice in Wonderland cliché. Discussion, argument, explanation, were all quite pointless. He was not interested. His mission was purely sadistic.

There came a point at which Tim excused himself, saying that he wanted to 'get on with the job on the front gate', and escaped, and X and I were alone amongst the teacups. He came, then, straight to the main charge; which was that a mutual friend in the Far East—in actual fact he hated the man's guts, and the other man had little use for him—had seen a letter I had written to a high-up government official out there in which I had said that my friendship with him, X, meant more to him than all his boys.

I said, wearily, that perhaps I had written that letter, but it was all fifteen years ago, and really I could not be expected to remember, but surely, anyhow, it was true? *Hadn't* our friendship been more important than all his one-night-stands with the native boys? I certainly hoped so. And there had never been any secret about his homosexuality, had there?

That was all very well in England, he declared, but *out there* it was different. If you were a foreigner you had to watch your step.

I could only suggest that it was a pity he hadn't written to me about it at the time; it was all so far away and long ago, now, fifteen years later. Had he really come all this way, after all this time, to pick such very old bones? Such very stale old bones... ?

He said, harshly, that he only wanted to 'get the record straight'. That old cliché; but he had always been addicted to clichés.

It is only three years ago, as I write this, but I do not remember how the conversation progressed from that point to the one at which I suggested that he might like to see 'the rest of the house'. He had got up from his armchair when Tim had left to go to the front gate and stood at the window, looking out into the garden, when he made the charge about the letter. That he was already on his feet made it possible to suggest the move, and I seized the opportunity it presented, for I know by long experience that if you want to get rid of a guest you must get that guest on the move. We went up to the study and he was interested in the Burmese Buddha that came via Ireland, and in a water-colour of the Shwe Dagon pagoda in Rangoon, but whilst I went on to explain how I had come by it I became aware that he was looking not at the picture but at the whisky decanter on a table in a corner of the room, and I remembered that he liked whisky, but you do not offer your enemy a drink. I wanted him gone, and showing him the house was merely a ruse to that end.

We left the study and went downstairs into the hall, and Sammy came in from the garden. X immediately bent down and picked him up. Sammy is a good-natured little feller and doesn't at all mind being picked up; in fact he likes it and switches on his built-in purr; but not this time, for X rubbed his fur up the wrong way, vigorously, and the more Sammy struggled to free himself the more vigorously he did this anti-cat thing.

'Please put him down!' I beseeched. 'He's hating it! Cats hate their fur being rubbed up the wrong way!'

In confirmation of this Sammy hissed and drove his sharp little teeth into the infuriating hand and X put him down and said, licking the blood from his hand, 'Very spoilt cat!' And then, 'Where did I leave my coat?'

I went into the sitting-room and took it from the back of the armchair and handed it to him. He asked, as he took it from me, 'Do you still get indigestion?'

'Indigestion?' I was startled, and then I remembered that 'out there' I had had a bout of it, and that we had stopped once at an English chemist's and I had bought some magnesia tablets. I added, 'I get it occasionally. Everyone does, I suppose. Why do you ask?'

'You don't *look* very well!' he said.

'I'm tired,' I said. 'I've done a lot of work lately. And I'm getting old.'

His smile was amused.

He offered no comment but said, only, 'I'll be on my way.'

We went out, then, through the front door and down the garden path to the front gate—which Tim had satisfactorily 'fixed', I noticed, as I opened it, but he himself was nowhere in sight. I asked X if he knew the way back to the railway station, and he said yes, he had noted some landmarks coming along in the taxi.

'You go straight ahead,' I said.

He looked ahead and I added, 'Goodbye.'

There was absolutely nothing else to say.

'Goodbye,' he said. He was no longer smiling, but cold.

We did not shake hands. He sauntered off up the road. Mission accomplished.

I went back up the path and into the house and Tim came in from the garden.

'Has he gone?' he asked, hopefully.

'Yes,' I said. 'I've just seen him off.'

'Thank goodness for that! He was so unpleasant. Really *nasty*! Why do you suppose he came?'

'Just to *be* unpleasant! Just to pick old bones. Fifteen-year-old bones.'

To come all out here just to pick such very stale old bones —what sort of venom was working in him, for God's sake?

But there was something working in him, for he died of cancer, in a London hospital, two years to the day on which he came here. I learned of it three days after his death.

Questions arise, but there are no answers. Something in him drove him to behave as he did. Some defect of personality. A kind of cancer of the spirit.

There is more to say, for I have thought much about it; but I will leave it there, as one of the uglier stories from my life. But sad, too. At the time it was horrible and hateful; in retrospect, with its tragic sequel, there attaches to it an infinite regret.

PART VI

Portrait of a Young Revolutionary
In Memoriam

I

Dissident Iraqis

Within a year of my long, late-night talk with General Abdel
Karim Qassim in the Ministry of Defence, in which he lived,
in Baghdad, early in 1962, and which I recorded in *A Lance
for the Arabs*, this 'son of Iraq', as he liked to call himself, was
shot in the music-room of the television building, as the finale
of the Ba'athist *coup* led by Colonel Abdul Salam Arif, on
Friday, 8 February, 1963, when the Ministry of Defence was
bombed by the Air Force Qassim had believed to be loyal to
him. In the Ministry he and his men fought it out literally to
the last bullet, and when they finally surrendered in the early
hours of the following morning, after Qassim had parleyed
with Arif by telephone—that Arif whose life he had once
spared—they knew they were going out to die, and by one-
thirty they were dead, Qassim and three others, including his
cousin, Fadhel Abbas Mahdawi, President of the People's
Court. The corpses were shown on television throughout the
rest of the day, over and over again, until, it seems, even people
who had not liked Qassim or the regime were sickened. The
handsome head of the 'Faithful Leader', as he had been until
that day when he became the 'Enemy of the People', was
held up by the hair, facing the cameras, so that all could see
that he was well and truly dead. Later in London I was shown
some of the stills. His face was bruised but he was handsome
still in death. I was shown these photographs by Khalid Zaki,
then President of the Iraqi Students' Society, who had written

to me following the publication of my letter to the *Daily Telegraph,** defending Qassim against the nonsense being talked
about him. I wrote that I had found him 'gentle and court-
eous, and a man of immense personal charm—as, to my knowledge, did many others who met him. He answered all my
questions simply and directly; he did not rant or harangue, and
he was so far removed from megalomania as to ask me
questions about myself, my background, etc. I did not find
anything abnormal in his manner, and I formed an impression
of deep sincerity.'

I added that I had toured Iraq extensively and found an
enormous amount being achieved under the Qassim regime—
'an active agrarian reform programme, with very considerable
distributions of land, and in addition to new schools and hospitals everywhere a very considerable housing programme.
The *sarifa,* the mud hovels of the very poor, were being abolished and the people moved into small modernly designed new
houses. The poor, whom he called his brothers, were Qassim's
special concern; this he expressed in his speeches, and to me
personally. I could, I concluded, put forward other points
in favour of this savagely maligned man, but offered only those
few, as an indication.

I came to learn a good deal more about him, later, and
realise the frustration he engendered in those who tried to
work with him, because of his idiosyncrasies and his perpetual
promising of a Constitution that never materialised; he was
ultimately the victim of his own good intentions—the road to
the television station music-room the day after that Black
Friday could be said to have been paved with them. But of
his sincerity there could be no doubt. He was a dreamer and
an idealist and should never have become involved in politics.
He should have stayed the soldier he was. I was shocked and
upset by his death, and always knew that one day I would
write his story; it took me five years to find a way to do it, but
in 1958 I wrote it in my novel, *The Midnight Street,* which is
virtually straight biography, with very little invented.

But in February, 1962, when my letter appeared in the
Daily Telegraph, five days after the tragic events of that

* February 13, 1963.

Black Friday, there was only the bitterness and anger and the despairing sense of frustration; this shocking thing had happened and there was nothing one could do about it. Abdel Karim Qassim had been shot like a dog, by order of his one-time friend and fellow-revolutionary, Abdul Salam Arif, who now reigned in his stead.

So that when shortly after my letter appeared in the *Daily Telegraph* the President of the Iraqi Students' Society in London contacted me it was a small spark of hope—not of being able to unseat Arif, of course not, but at least of being able to do something for Arif's numerous political prisoners—the Communists and 'Qassimites'. Qassim was not a Communist; he could be described, I suppose, as a sentimental socialist; in the 1958 revolution which he and Arif made together, and which overthrew the monarchy and established the Republic of Iraq, he had the support of the Communists; within a year he had fallen out with them; after refusing them seats in the Cabinet, and the attempt on his life in May, 1959, after which he was hospitalised for two months, has been variously blamed on Communists and Nasserists. What ever is the truth of that, Qassim used the Communists at the outset, and there was a sense in which they used—or attempted to use—him. Now they would use his death. From the beginning I realised that some of the 'Qassimite' Iraqi students who became my colleagues were Communists, but I was glad of an opportunity to work against the Arif regime, and the cause of political prisoners anywhere has always been one close to my heart. I am anyhow not 'anti-Communist'; as I see it, true Communism, like true Christianity, could be a very good thing; what I am opposed to is the element of dictatorship and brain-washing that invades Communism in practice; it need not, but it unfortunately does.

Thus, when Khalid Zaki wrote to me I was not concerned as to whether he was a Communist or not; it was enough for me that he was a 'Qassimite'. He asked whether I would come along to the premises of the Iraqi Students' Society in Shavers Place, off Leicester Square, where was also the office of the Bertrand Russell Foundation, with which he was associated, for a talk. I immediately telephoned and fixed a date.

Shavers Place is what my friend of the Windsor journey would call not much of a 'hood'. It is old and shabby and no doubt ripe for 'development'. There are overflowing dustbins, steep, dark narrow stairs, doors dubiously inscribed—'Photographer's Model'—grimy-looking w.c.s indecently exposed on landings—a smell of tomcats and garbage and drains. Perhaps it is better now; perhaps it no longer exists; but that is how it was then—ten years ago.

I passed what appeared to be the newly-painted doors of the Bertrand Russell Foundation and toiled on up to a scruffy door inscribed Iraqi Students' Society. I knocked and entered and found myself in a small room in which a dozen or so dark-haired, darkish-skinned young men, and a few similarly dark girls, sat round in a semi-circle on the kind of chairs used at meetings; a young man who was addressing them broke off as I entered. I murmured Good-evening and don't-let-me-disturb-you and seated myself on a vacant chair next to a startled but smiling girl. They were all evidently startled and astonished, but I merely assumed that I had arrived a little early, before they were ready for me, and wondered vaguely which of them was Khalid Zaki, and then the one who had been addressing the group addressed himself to me, to inquire, politely, 'Who did you wish to see, please?'

'I have an appointment with Khalid Zaki,' I told him.

'Ah, yes. He is expecting you. If you will come with me, please...'

I was conducted across the landing to a very small room full of filing cabinets, where another dark-haired young man sat at a table littered with paper.

He looked up as we entered then rose to his feet, smiling—a smile of most singular warmth.

'You are Miss Ethel Mannin?' he inquired eagerly.

'Yes.'

We shook hands and the other young man withdrew.

Khalid pulled a chair forward from somewhere and we faced each other across the cluttered table. He came straight to the point. He and other friends in the Society had been discussing with Mr. Will Griffiths, the Labour M.P., the idea of forming a committee to help the many people who had been imprisoned since the *coup*, and if possible to send a fact-finding commission out to Baghdad. Mr. Will Griffiths was an old friend of Iraqi students in London, since 1955, when they were protesting against the Nuri es Said regime, and he was very willing to help now. It was proposed to meet with Mr. Will Griffiths, and other sympathetic Labour M.P.s, at the House of Commons, and if I also was interested . . .

The dark eyes glowed with eagerness.

I said that of course I was, but could such a committee hope to be effective?

He declared that it could be and would be; a British committee would carry a lot of weight in Iraq because of Britain's special relationship with the country; there had been the British Mandate, and there were still the British oil interests.

We talked and were joined later by others. I apologised for barging in on their meeting, but they laughed and said I was welcome, I was their good friend.

So began the friendship which was to last for the rest of Khalid Zaki's life—five years.

He was then twenty-three.

At the first meeting at the House of Commons the British Committee for the defence of Human Rights in Iraq was formed, with Lord Chorley, the Labour peer, as Chairman, Will Griffiths as Secretary, and myself as Treasurer. A distinguished list of sponsors included Lord Boyd-Orr, many Labour M.P.s, amongst whom was my old friend and fellow-campaigner of many causes for freedom and justice since the late thirties, Fenner Brockway.

We sent out appeals for money and met with a generous response from local Labour Parties, Trades Councils, and individuals, including impecunious Iraqi students. We were soon financially in the position to send out the commission we planned in an attempt to secure first-hand information as to what was going on; it was hoped that the commission would get into the prisons and interview political and other prisoners, and when it was claimed that people who had been imprisoned without trial since the *coup* were now free, to verify this—that they were in fact alive and well. Our plan was to send our Secretary, Will Griffiths, and Leslie Hale, M.P.—an experienced and able lawyer—and an Iraqi of our own choosing to act as guide and interpreter. But in a series of interviews with the then Acting Chargé d'Affaires at the Iraqi embassy we were met with the repeated refusal to accept our selected Iraqi colleague as part of the commission. The embassy was prepared to issue visas to the M.P.s if they went alone, prepared on their arrival in Baghdad to accept an Iraqi guide and interpreter provided by the Foreign Office there. This, for obvious reasons, was totally unacceptable to the Committee. We debated the idea of the M.P.s going out alone and coping as best they could when they got there, independently of any Government-selected escort, but decided that it would not achieve the objects we had in mind.

Whilst we were in this quandary, still hoping against hope to find an Iraqi who might be willing to accompany the commission and who would be acceptable to the embassy, Will Griffiths, with five other Labour M.P.s, was invited by the Iraqi Government to Baghdad. This was a piece of great good fortune for the Committee, since it would not cost us anything, and although as part of a government-sponsored delegation of this kind it would not be possible to do all we had in mind, on the principle that something is always better than nothing the Committee was very glad for its Secretary to go in this way and do for us what he could—which, as it turned out, was a good deal. The Committee was further fortunate in receiving an offer from Leslie Hale to fly on to Baghdad after a visit to Kenya for the independence celebrations and do what he could for us. This he did, and as a one-man fact-finding commission did a fine job, succeeding in interviewing various political prisoners, in addition to pursuing effectively a number of inquiries.

The valuable reports brought back from Baghdad by Will Griffiths and Leslie Hale were issued by the Committee in the form of a booklet, for which I wrote the preface; we called it, simply, *Report from Iraq*; we brought it out in February, 1964; the M.P.s were in Baghdad in October, 1963. The reports confirmed that the stories which had reached us of imprisonments without trial, of both men and women, and of torture, were not exaggerated.

What the British Committee asked was that all political prisoners be either released or quickly brought to trial; that the war in Iraqi Kurdistan cease, in favour of peaceful negotiation; and that fighter 'planes and arms should not be supplied to the Iraqi Government by the British Government for use against the Kurds.

To this end, as a result of our frequent sessions in a committee room at the House of Commons, we sent cables to President Arif and kept up our campaign here, issuing Information Bulletins and getting letters into the press when possible, and in February, 1965, we convened in London an International Conference on a General Amnesty for Iraqi Political Prisoners, at which delegates from four continents attended, with Members of Parliament of various countries, trade union leaders, and an opening address by Bertrand Russell speaking in the name of the Bertrand Russell Peace Foundation.

At the close of the two-day conference we sent a letter to the United Nations urging the demand for an Amnesty, and to President Nasser urging him to use his influence with Arif to this end.

2

Khalid

In all this Khalid Zaki and I met not only at the committee meetings at the House of Commons but at Oak Cottage, where we worked together on the Information Bulletins issued by the Committee. They were curious occasions because although there was mutual liking and a developing affection between us we never, ever, discussed anything but Iraq. Thus we never knew anything about each other as human beings. He knew something about me as a writer but nothing about me as a person other than the bare biographical facts; I, similarly, knew only the biographical—which of course included the political—facts about him. He knew that I had a daughter; I knew that he had a brother—indeed, he once brought this brother to the house, but though we sat round the dining-room table and enjoyed food and wine together we still only talked Iraq. What was his private life, if any, whether he had a girl friend, what he did in his leisure moments, if any, I had no idea. Between his work for the Committee, his work as a student, and his work at the Bertrand Russell Peace Foundation, which provided him with a living when he ceased to be a student, he could have had almost no spare time. He could not return to Iraq because, as a Communist, the embassy in London withheld his passport.

This withholding of passports was a source of intense bitterness and resentment amongst a number of Iraqi students here, but there was nothing that they or anyone else could do about it; for Khalid the situation became serious when there was some doubt about whether his permit to remain here would be renewed. There was an evening when he and Will Griffiths and I left the House of Commons together, after a Committee meeting, when Khalid, usually so sanguine, was worried and depressed. That night, for some reason, we did not leave as we usually did by the St. Stephen's entrance but came out into the courtyard, under Big Ben. I have always remembered looking up at that great four-sided clock-face, glowing like the moon against the sky's darkness, and the curious sensation of never having been so close to it before, and that it boomed ten o'clock as we passed under it. I can never see Big Ben at night now without recalling that sensation, and Khalid's unwontedly dark mood. Within a few days, he morosely declared, unless something happened about his permit, he could be put on a 'plane and sent back to Baghdad, where he would be arrested at the airport. Will Griffiths and I assured him that this would not happen; that we would not allow it to happen. It didn't happen, of course, and I think it was due to Will Griffiths' efforts to that end at the Home Office, but it was the only time I ever saw Khalid despondent. It was intensely important to him that he should remain in London until such time as it suited his revolutionary purpose to leave it. He would get back to Baghdad when he was ready to—illegally, via Prague.

But before then there was the Paris Conference, a year after the London one, and which he very much wanted me to attend, but which I did not attend, feeling nervously exhausted at that time. I was working on a difficult non-fiction book, *Loneliness, a study of the human condition,** and also had the proofs of the second Palestine novel, *The Night and its Homing,*† on hand. I felt unequal to making the Paris effort, and also I had no real faith in its usefulness.

Khalid was in Paris, Prague, Cairo, Rome, in 1965, making 'contacts' for the London Conference, and then later in the year for the Paris one; in lieu of a passport he always managed to get 'travel documents' for wherever he wanted to go.

* 1966.
† 1966.

I received postcards and letters from him on his journeyings. From Paris in January, 1965, I received a letter from him
in which he reported success in meeting some important
journalists, including one from *Le Monde*, and some French
writers; all attached great importance to the forthcoming
London Conference, he wrote, and he hoped that Will
Griffiths and I would play an important part in it. He was
going to Rome in two days' time, was waiting for his visa for
Cairo, and would probably go to Lebanon as well. There was
nothing personal in his letter except his 'deep affections'. He
was in Paris again in September, and sent me a coloured picture postcard of the Pont Alexandre on which he referred,
derisively, to 'another *coup*' in Iraq, which proved again, he
said, 'our estimation of the situation there.' He hoped that the
Bulletin was 'under control'. . . .

A coloured postcard of the Sphinx and Pyramids from
Cairo reported the weather 'warm and lovely', and that things
were going *almost* well there. I never, really, understand the
italicised almost.

Whilst in Prague he had 'bought' me a coffee-service, with
which he was very pleased, and he was sure I would like it; in
fact it had been paid for by Dr. Naziha Dulaimi—a former
minister in the Qassim government, and sentenced to death
in absentia after the 1963 *coup*—because he himself, he wrote
cheerfully, had no money. Dr. Dulaimi would bring it with
her when she came to London in February for the Conference.
I duly received the coffee set, and it proved to be very decora-
tive in its modernistic fashion, but not, really, very practical,
the cups being too thick and shallow, yet it remains one of
my most treasured possessions.

Before he left for Paris in 1967 he came out to Oak Cottage
in a car with some Iraqi friends, bringing all his books for me
to keep for him. We stacked them all in a corner of the dining-
room; there were a great many Marxist works, in English,
and, surprisingly, some tattered paperbacks of thrillers—but
these, he said, were his brother's; they had shared the flat. It
was a bright warm summer day and he was very happy, all
smiles, cheerfulnesss, energy. He didn't know when he'd be
back to collect the books, but he would be back, for sure. When

he returned to the car with his friends we just shook hands and I wished him luck. There was no dramatic sense of leave-taking; he would write, he said, and he did . . . even, eventually, from Baghdad.

We had discussed about writing; he would not, of course, sign the letters once he had left Paris, and he would use a 'code' when necessary; I would have to read between the lines —wasn't that the English expression? If, for example, he wrote that the weather was very fine I would know that things were going well, and *vice-versa*. The letters from Iraq would not, of course, come by post, but be posted in London by this person and that; people came and went; it was not too difficult.

In Paris he would grow a moustache, and a small beard to hide the identity mark of the mole on his chin; then he would acquire a passport. I gathered that given the right contacts this, also, was not difficult. I never asked him questions, and I assumed that when he had achieved his illegal return to Baghdad he would work with the underground Communist movement against the regime. I did not see this as being effective, and had once suggested to him that the Arif regime would only be toppled in the way it had come to power—that is to say as the result of a military *coup*. He smiled and said that a military *coup* was one thing, revolution another; he was interested in revolution. There had been revolution in Iraq in 1958, when the monarchy had been overthrown; there could be revolution again. What had happened in 1963 was not a revolution; it was merely a *coup*. With this, of course, I entirely agreed, and I remember this conversation very well, for I said that I hoped when he and his comrades had achieved their revolution they would not repeat the pattern of imprisonments and executions. I remember very clearly that I said, firmly, 'There have been enough killings!' And I remember how he stared at me, his dark eyes intent, and exclaimed, incredulously, 'You would not *kill* anyone?' To which I replied, 'I would not kill anyone—not even Arif!'

At that he laughed, assuming, I think, that I had only been joking all along. But I meant what I said; and so did he mean what he did not say in so many words but very clearly implied —that there did just naturally have to be killings. It was part of the pattern of revolution. He enormously admired Che Guevara. As I do. I admire the courage, selflessness, and dedication of guerillas everywhere, whilst regretting their tactics, and, on the pragmatic level, I do not see these tactics succeeding.

Well, then, so Khalid went off laughing to Paris, on his way to Prague and Baghdad, and on December 23, 1967, there was a Christmas card purchased at the Dar Al-Hikmah bookshop in Baghdad, a gay card, in imitation needlework, of the heads of a boy and a girl biting into hunks of water-melon; he wrote inside that he 'strongly hoped' we should meet in 1968, and that 'our plans are going forward', and 'I will make sure that we will not lose contact in the future'. This, I think, was a reference to a long silence before the Christmas card. He thanked me for my letter, and sent best wishes to my daughter.

There was a letter in the new year, in reply to mine thanking for the Christmas card; in it he wrote that he was leaving Baghdad and going to somewhere 'more dangerous, but more useful'.

The next news I had was six months later, of his death in the south of Iraq, in May, he and five other young men, in 'an armed clash with the police and the Army'.

He would by then have been about twenty-eight years old.

3

The Marshes

On 15 April, 1966, I was in California, staying with my old friend, Rickey Austin, at his ranch in Pauma Valley. He had driven into Escondido for provisions and newspapers, and on his return told me, 'There's something in the news that will interest you—a statesman in Iraq has been killed in an air-crash.' I inquired, hopefully, 'The President?' But he hadn't read the report; only glanced at the headlines, and he didn't remember. He handed me a copy of *The New York Times*. I seized it eagerly, and there the good news was—President Abdel Salam Arif had been killed in a helicopter crash in the desert the day before, on a flight to Basra, in the south, and 'it was attributed by Baghdad radio to a sandstorm'.

I wondered if it was in fact a sandstorm that caused the crash. Later, back in London, I was told by Iraqis that there was no sandstorm in the desert on that day. It could have been sabotage by dissident Kurds. It could have been, and it was a nice idea, but Khalid laughed and discounted it. He was afraid, he said, that it was just an accident. Arif had gone; but what difference did it make? Now there was his brother, Arif II. In all nine men had died in the crash. It began to seem less of a nice idea. And, as Khalid had been so quick to point out, so far as the regime went it made no difference.

By that time the British Committee had virtually ceased to exist. After the London Conference an International Continuing Committee was formed to implement the results of the

Conference and continue the campaign for the release of the Iraqi political prisoners, but I had felt unable to serve on this Committee, and my recollection of it was that it was somehow lost in the Bertrand Russell Foundation, for which Khalid was still working—though I was never clear what he did there; he worked with Ralph Schoenmann, the American who was then Russell's secretary. He liked and admired Khalid, and Khalid, I think, reciprocated the affection.

But Khalid's great friend in London was a Kurdish student with whom I also became very friendly, and we worked together on the Bulletins put out by the British Committee—for me he was by way of being Khalid's deputy. It was from him that I learned in August, 1968, of Khalid's death in the south of Iraq in May—the news was a curiously long time in reaching here, and it was not until months later, when I met Khalid's brother here that I learned the details, and that Khalid and his comrades had in fact been killed in the marshes in the Basra area, where they had been attempting to raise a Che Guevara style revolt against the regime. This was the 'more dangerous but more useful' area of which he had written me in that last letter. He had had hopes of that area because the people there were poor, just as Che had had hopes of the poor Bolivian peasants.

I had been in Basra in 1962, and had been taken out in a flat-bottomed boat into the reed-filled marshes. I have a chapter on the marshes in *A Lance for the Arabs*, and wrote in it of the jungles of reeds. In those jungles Khalid and his friends died; the Army sent in helicopters to search them out.

It took the Zaki family in Baghdad some time to recover Khalid's body from the authorities in Basra for burial in Baghdad, Khalid's brother told me . . . amongst other distressing details I would rather not have known. Later he sent me some post-mortem pictures—at which I could not bear to look; I sent them to his Kurdish friend, warning him as to their nature, but it seemed he liked to have them. I have the little passport picture Khalid gave me in 1965, inscribed 'to my dear friend', and it depicts him as I remember him, with his warm smile, at the House of Commons committee meetings, in the garden here when we sat drafting bulletins instead of relaxing in the sunshine and chatting lightly as friends do. We were good friends, and the affection was deep and it was mutual, yet we never knew each other very well—as human beings.

I gave all his books eventually to the Iraqi Students' Society, and the day they were put into cartons and carried down the garden path to the car belonging to the Iraqi friend who had come for them was somehow the real farewell, more poignant, because more personal, than the memorial service held for him at the Conway Hall in London and at which I spoke, likening him, inevitably, to Che Guevara. Well, he was in that tradition, all right, and his death as tragic; and as futile. Guevara had at least a chance of success—according to Fidel Castro, who wrote the introduction to the published *Diary,* a good chance—but Khalid Zaki and his friends had none; it was perhaps the purest political romanticism; it was certainly political idealism.

It is true, I suppose, that Ernesto Che Guevara was the most courageous, dedicated and brilliant revolutionary of our time; whether Khalid Zaki, who modelled himself on Che, had the same brilliance is debatable; certainly he had the same courage and dedication. Perhaps his death in the marshes was not quite futile; perhaps it is true, as Castro maintains, that the guerilla is always a catalyst.

N

PART VII
The Continuing Story

I

Three-Score-Years-and-Ten

Not long before his seventieth birthday my father, ever
fanciful, being of Irish stock, dreamed, so he told me, that
Death had tapped him on the shoulder and said, 'Bob Mannin, I want you!' My father was in no wise dismayed by this
dream, for three-score-years-and-ten seemed ample to him,
and he often talked, cheerfully, about his journey across the
River Styx, as though it were some sort of one-way excursion.
In spite of this dream, however, Bob Mannin had another
five-and-a-half years to go—before he died after five weeks in
a London hospital; on the morning of Christmas Eve, with a
Christmas tree at the foot of his bed . . . as I have told in my
little monograph about him, written three years after his death,
in an attempt to ease my still grieving heart, *This Was a Man.**
I gave the money from this little book to an East London
youth club I was interested in at the time and of which Bob
Mannin would have approved, being himself a Cockney, born
in a Westminster slum, and fantastically generous—he who
all his life had so very little. I doubt if they come like that
nowadays, in the affluent society; and the Westminster slum
has long been a most expensive and fashionable little
street; as has the Westminster 'terrace' in which my parents
had a 'maisonette' when they were first married, my father
having graduated by then from being a Covent Garden
market porter to a sorter in the inland section of Mount
Pleasant General Post Office, the which he was for forty years,

* 1952.

until his retirement at the age of sixty. He always said that the day he retired he would spit on the doorstep of Mount Pleasant, and I hope he did.

But I did not set out in this chapter to rewrite the monograph of my father but to consider this business of three-score-years-and-ten, to achieve which it is only necessary to live long enough, and which nowadays is not considered at all a remarkable achievement, though, to be sure, a considerable amount of 'flap' can attach to the seventieth birthday of anyone famous enough and in good standing with the 'media'. The ninetieth psalm is a prayer of Moses, in which he declared that 'we spend our years as a tale that is told', adding that 'the days of our years are three score and ten; and if by reason of strength they be fourscore years, yet is their strength labour and sorrow . . .' But Moses was 'an hundred and twenty years old when he died', and 'his eye was not dim, nor his natural force abated', as is set forth in the Fifth Book of Moses, called *Deuteronomy*, in the seventh verse of the thirty-fourth chapter. He died in the plain of Moab, after having seen the Promised Land from the top of Pisgah, 'over against Jericho', and the Lord said, 'I have caused thee to see it with thine eyes, but thou shalt not go over'.

So Moses had not three-score-years-and-ten but twice three score, which would seem to most people nowadays about twice too much. Yet with what gusto in our youth did some of us declare with Ulysses that 'life piled on life were all too little!' Strange, most strange, it seems, when the fire sinks low that it could ever have blazed so fiercely.

I write this shortly after completing my three-score-years-and-twelve. A certain shock, I think, attaches to one's seventieth birthday—the shock of the realisation that one has had one's 'allotted span', and anything that comes after that is a bonus. It seems so very far-away-and-long-ago that we were young-and-twenty, and yet, too, it has all gone so incredibly quickly. Well, but there you are; you've had your allotted span and you're still there—and for all you know there may be another ten, fifteen, or even twenty years of it, which is a daunting thought.

When W. Somerset Maugham wrote in his autobiographical volume, *The Summing Up*, published in 1938, that he looked forward to old age without dismay he was sixty-four, and he wrote that he felt the future was 'so short'; he had in fact still a long way to go—nearly another thirty years; he died on December 15, 1965, by which time he was ninety-one and had lived too long. As far back as 1938 he sometimes longed for death, he wrote, as the 'final and absolute freedom', and would be 'drunk with the thought of it'. Even so he was willing enough to go on living, he declared, so long as the doctors could keep him in tolerable health. His end was wretched, all the same; and some of it deplorable; it all went on too long. In his last book, a volume of essays, *Points of View*, published in 1958, just over sixty years after his first, his novel, *Liza of Lambeth*, he declared, writing of Goethe, 'what makes old age hard to bear is not the failing of one's faculties, mental and physical, but the burden of one's memories'. Maugham was eighty-four when he wrote that, and he knew. Twenty years earlier he had been able to write of the positive compensations of old age, chiefest of which was the liberation from the 'trammels of human egoism', making it possible to enjoy art and literature 'without the bias that in youth warps the judgement'. In old age, too, he could write then, we were no longer the 'slaves of passion', and was it so small thing to be liberated from their sway, he asked; it was 'something to be free from the pangs of unrequited love and the torment of jealousy'.

It *is*, of course, no mean thing to be liberated from all that anguish of what Ortega y Gasset calls the 'erotic seizure', and to be no longer causing unhappiness to other people in pursuit of the fulfilment of that seizure; listening, sympathetically, to the tales of others still so tormented it is impossible not to be glad that one is 'done with all that'. But there is this also to be said—that the arid fact remains that when one's sexuality is dead all that is most vital in oneself is dead. It is a sombre thought. The anguish and the ecstasy are inseparable; in that experience you knew yourself alive; to suffer was to live. Old age knows love and sorrow, but no ecstasy; its love has nothing whatever to do with sex but everything to do with deep caring and concern; it is concentrated within the intimate circle of the family and very old friends; the sorrow is part of that deep concern, and the sorrow of death as those near and dear drop out along the long road—the end of which is near, yet always hidden round the next corner; mercifully.

When I was young-and-twenty I was tremendously impressed by the fact that the famous courtesan, Ninon de Lenclos, reputedly had a lover at seventy. This seemed to me quite fabulous. Could it really be so, I asked myself, awed—a woman of *seventy*, when even *forty* was old-and-done-for? (Those were the days when one exclaimed, impatiently of a young-middle-aged woman, 'Good heavens, she's *forty* if she's a day!' There was still half a lifetime to go before one would say, mildly, 'After all, she's only forty!') By the time I was seventy myself I had long been liberated from the erotic seizure, but Madame de Lenclos was in it for the money, so if she hadn't by then made enough to retire on who should blame her? Though, of course, she might simply have enjoyed her work. When I was told, fairly recently, by an old friend now in his eighties that his last *affaire* had been when he was eighty, with a woman of seventy-three, who, he said, had thoroughly enjoyed the occasion, my reaction was one of distaste; even, to be quite honest, of disapproval. I would rather not have known. By modern standards, I suppose, the attitude is puritanical. Certainly if two elderly people wish to behave in such a way, and are capable of it, and give pleasure to each other, there is, rationally, nothing against it. Yet it turns me sideways with distaste; I find it undignified, ludicrous—in a word, *unseemly*.

The human male takes a pride in sustaining virility until late in life; the human female seems not to have this kind of sexual vanity; I have anyhow never met an elderly woman who boasted of continuing sexual prowess, whereas I have met a number of men, and there are the recorded cases of the famous, such as Goethe, who at seventy-three had a passion for a girl of seventeen and even aspired to marry her, and Michelangelo who at sixty passionately loved a beautiful young man, to whom he addressed a number of impassioned sonnets, one of which he unequivocally entitled, *Love's Flame Doth Feed on Age*, in which he demanded:

> '*If some mild heat of love in youth confessed*
> *Burns a fresh heart with swift consuming fire,*
> *What will the force be of a flame more dire*
> *Shut up within an old man's cindery breast?*'

This he answered with a rhetorical question in the last three lines of the sonnet :

> '*A little flame consumed and fed on me*
> *In my green age; now that the wood is dry,*
> *What hope against this fire more fierce have I?*'*

When sexual passion does thus linger on into old age it is surely not a consummation devoutly to be desired, but, on the contrary, a condition to be pitied. There should surely be porte after the stormie seas of youth. *That*, surely, is the consummation devoutly to be desired? Well, it seemed so to W. Somerset Maugham, and it seems so to me.

Maugham, writing when he was sixty-four, could find compensations in old age other than liberation from sexual bondage; it is much to be doubted whether he found any when it really happened to him—which in one's sixties it hasn't. The sixties are a long way from being even middle-aged, but, also, are not-all-that-old. The sexual *sturm ünd drang* is over—for most people, anyhow—but plenty of physical energy remains on other levels. Or so I found in that decade. I spent my sixty-third birthday sitting on a rock in the Nubian desert, in a temperature of 120° F, waiting for the dirty little steamer to come down the Nile from Wadi Halfa for Aswan—nobody knew when. I was sitting on the rock, out in the open, with the sun vertically overhead—which in the Tropic of Cancer it very soon is—because under the few scrawny thorn trees no space remained in the thin shade, so many villagers there were waiting, with their bundles, for that steamer for the no less fiery furnace of Aswan.

Of that Nubian nightmare, in villages where the only water was the Nile, which you drank neat, I have written in *Aspects of Egypt*† and my novel, *The Burning Bush*,‡ and I mention

* Translation by J. A. Symonds, 1878.
† 1964.
‡ 1965.

it here only in the context of what is still physically possible in the sixties. I became ill with amoebic dysentery—not from drinking neat Nile but from the amoebea carried by the flies, the Egyptian doctor in Cairo told me—and a degree of dehydration, with no sweat in that intense heat, no saliva, only a bitter taste in the mouth and cracked lips, and almost no urine; but in the capable hands of the Cairo doctor I quickly recovered; now in the seventies I doubt whether I could survive such a trip, and have certainly no slightest desire to undertake one.

All my Middle East travels were in the first half of the sixties, as I have indicated—I did not get to that area until I was sixty-two. I went on my third and last visit to the U.S.A., by ship, and alone, tourist class, in the spring of 1966, when I was sixty-five. I did the coast to coast journey from New York City to Los Angeles by Greyhound coach, which takes three days and three nights, and adds up to a very long 'bus ride, and, since you cannot lie down in the coach, a big backache. It produced a travel book, *An American Journey*,* and two novels with Californian backgrounds, *The Lady and the Mystic*,† and *Bitter Babylon*,‡ and was the last big journey I did, and I shall do no more. Enough is enough.

But the sixties are all right; there is plenty of physical energy left; the seventies are another matter. The sixties, really, are a kind of transitional period from middle-age to old age.

The continuing story is of the seventies.

* 1967.
† 1967.
‡ 1968.

2

The Quiet Rhythm

The days are very quiet, now; uneventful; but that is all right; it is, in fact, the way I like it. My idea of a good day is when I haven't to go anywhere and no one is coming. I like to see people occasionally, and people do come here, because I invite them, old friends, and a few newly-acquired young friends, and I produce simple meals, and there is always wine, and we sit and talk—of books, of people, of the world political scene, and this I like. But less and less do I much want to go anywhere, and my favourite poem is one by Henry Reed, called *A Good Dream*, which is about not-going . . .

*'And the vanishing birds and embowered air gave me to know
That I was free of something and need not go . . .'*

I know, now, that I should never make engagements far ahead, for when the time comes more likely than not I won't want to keep them, and if possible will extricate myself; there will come upon me a sense of overwhelming relief in the realisation that *I need not go.* That I *need* not go.

But once in a way I make an effort and up-and-go somewhere, as when in June, 1971, I went to Paris for a couple of days to see my old friend, Rickey Austin, over from California, as I have recounted. Sometimes, though not very often, I go into town, to the London that has long ceased to be the city I once knew and had affection for, but uglified now by high-rise buildings, and monstrous with traffic and pollution. I go in to meet my publisher and discuss this and that, collect proofs, look at the rough drawings of a book jacket; very occasionally I go in for a theatre, or an exhibition of paintings. I am no longer interested in lunching or dining-out, much preferring a snack-lunch in a pub or a wine-bar, or an evening meal at the home of a friend. I do not want to go to parties or receptions any more—all that standing about; the babble, and the noise; and the futility. Something no longer to be borne; and splendidly I know that I am 'free of something and need not go. . . .'

Having long ceased to be interested in 'clothes' there is no question of going to town for shopping; an interest in clothes for their own sake belongs, like the wearing of perfume, to a life in which *l'amour* has a part; when it no longer has a part then perfume becomes superfluous and clothes are bought only when really needed and then with an eye to practicality rather than any consideration of fashion or elegance. For everyday purposes it is hardly necessary to be more than clean-and-tidy; for 'going out' one hopes to be presentable—that is to say at least not shabby or frowsy. There are people who retain an interest in clothes all their lives; my mother, who lived to be eighty-five, did; whereas my father never had it at any time, regarding clothes as just something to cover your nakedness, and exasperating my poor mother thereby; it was something she could never understand or be reconciled to. She admired men who were well-groomed; who looked 'smart', and she was married to a man who did not care in the least if he was mis-taken for a tramp. My own interest in clothes finished some-where in the middle sixties. I still wear the 'burglar suit' made some fourteen years or so ago from Reginald's, after his death; fortunately, being tailored in the 'classic' manner it has not dated, and Irish tweed lasts almost forever. I like old clothes, anyhow; like old books they become old friends.

I like, too, the rhythm of an orderly routine. For many years now I have worked at night; the mornings are occupied with domesticity—shopping, and, on the mornings when I don't walk up to the 'village' with my shopping basket, with odds and ends of chores about the house—I have had no domestic help for years; the afternoons are devoted to correspondence, which flows in with tidal regularity; after tea and the six o'clock news there is a routine telephone conversation with an old friend—very often the only conversation of the day—and then, after seven, unless I can think of some other reason for postponing it, a start has to be made on work, which usually begins with reading through what I wrote the night before and deciding that a good deal of it won't do. By midnight I have usually made some progress, however, with a thousand words or so on paper, which, with some revision of the previous night's work, is fair enough, and, maintained steadily, for five nights a week, means, even with all the rewriting, that at the end of four or five months you have a book.

In my youth I worked in the day time; I had resident domestic help, and the nights were given over to all manner of gaieties; working at night began with that sobering-up period of the end of the thirties, of which I wrote in *Young in the Twenties*,* and which flowed into the blacked-out nights of the war years. After the war I worked a good deal by lamplight in the Connemara cottage. Now even if circumstances permitted of it I could not work in the day time. I like the quietness of night, the sense of seclusion behind the closed curtains and the world shut out. It's a solitary life, and lonely. It is also very exhausting.

Writing a book, whether fiction or non-fiction, is a hard slog of unremittingly sustained effort, mental and physical, and more of a slog as you grow older and have less mental and physical energy to bring to bear, plus the handicap of a greater self-criticism, causing you to forbear to fling words on to paper any old how just so long as it got set-down, as in the youthful fire of creativity. When you are old writing becomes an arduous, and even a disagreeable business, as writers more distinguished than I am—and notably Graham Greene—have observed. Why those not driven by economic necessity go on with it I simply do not know; perhaps it becomes a habit, and like 'God' in the Calman cartoon, they would like to retire, 'but what would I do?' I am filled with awe when I read that Agatha Christie wrote a novel in five weeks when she was

* 1971.

seventy-eight. When I was thirty-six I wrote a novel in six weeks, *Rose and Sylvie*, a study of juvenile delinquency based on an actual case of which I had read in a newspaper, and which had interested me from the psychological angle; I had never before, and have never since, written a novel in that time, and could only do so then because I was away from home and had nothing else to do, and it was, in any case, a very easy novel to write—simple and uncomplicated, and in a sense journalistic. But I know a best-selling novelist now in his eighties who assured me that he doesn't find writing, now, any easier or harder than he ever did. I can only admire and envy such vitality.

In the twenty years between his autobiography, *The Summing Up*, and his last book, *Points of View*, a volume of essays, Somerset Maugham wrote a good many short stories, but only three or four novels, of which *Catalina*, published in 1948, when he was seventy-four, was his last. He had always a preference for short stories, because, as he explains in *The Summing Up*, you do not get as 'sick of' the characters in the two or three weeks it may take to write a story as during the months you have to spend in their company when writing a novel. I was interested that he declared that 'most writers have chills and fevers, aches and pains, nausea at times, when they are engaged in composition'. Conrad was invariably unwell when writing a novel and in a state of collapse at the end. Some of us, on the other hand, are so thankful to have the damn thing finished at long and weary last that when it is we feel a whole lot better.

Sammy-cat was part of the quiet rhythm of my present days. If he was not around when I opened the front door at about eight-thirty in the morning to take in the paper and the letters I would leave a door open and he would come in later, and if I was still in bed he would come upstairs and jump up on to the bed, very friendly and affectionate, and quite content to wait for his breakfast until I got up for the second time to turn on the bath and brace myself for another day—feeling in the mornings very much in sympathy with Emily Dickinson in her cry for help as expressed in her poem—'*A day! Help! Help! Another day!*' When the sun shone Sammy would spend

most of the day outside; on other days on a chair beside my
typing desk—though occasionally in my wire basket, so that
I must pull the letters out from under him, or make the excuse
not to answer them that day because the cat was sitting on
them. When I brought my tea tray up to the study at about
five-thirty he would sit up, have a wash-and-brush-up, then
walk along the typing desk, along the narrow cat-walk in
front of the machine, and on to the flap extended at the righthand side. Here he would sit waiting to be carried downstairs
—it was a 'thing' with him developed only in the last year.
When I got up he also got up and reached his fore-paws up to
my shoulder. I would pick him up and he would cling tightly,
pushing his head against my face and purring. Thus affectioned
we would descend to the kitchen, where he would weave around
my legs whilst I assembled his supper, then, with two saucers on
an old tray we would go out through the dining-room and on
to a covered loggia where I would leave him his food, come
back into the house, closing the door behind me, and return
to the study and the night's work. Later he might have gone
round the house to sit on the coal-bin by the kitchen door
waiting patiently for a second helping. Sometimes he would
be there at midnight, hopeful of a late-night snack.

But now there is no more Sammy.

I do no writing at the weekends but, weather permitting,
work in the garden. It is a large and beautiful old garden,
terraced, with lily-ponds and rose-beds and borders, and a belt
of tall elms at the top of a grassy slope above the loggia, and
rhododendrons and magnolias, and a bit of woodland which
in May becomes a bluebell wood. From the first snowdrops on
the slope in February, through the succession of crocuses and
bluebells, to the cherry-blossom and the crab-apple, to the
azaleas and rhododendrons, the lilies-of-the-valley and the
wistaria—no Japanese gardens, even at Kyōto, ever produced
finer—to the first flush of roses in June—and there are over
fifty varieties and well over a hundred bushes—down to the
second flush in September, and some of the floribunda still at
it into late November—it is a quite uniquely beautiful garden,
so that newcomers, stepping out on to the loggia exclaim, won-

deringly, 'It's like being in the country!' In my youth, in the twenties and thirties, I did just naturally have a gardener, just as one did just naturally have domestic help, resident at that— 'maids', cook-generals, cook-housekeepers—but for the last twenty years or so my only help has been at weekends, when Tim and I work together in the garden, weather permitting, though there are, of course, weekends when other friends are here, and then little or no gardening gets done. It is all, nevertheless, kept in good order, the grass cut, the rosebeds and borders hoed, the paths weeded, and in due season the Battle of the Leaves valiantly waged—and incidentally we make very good leaf-mould, which we use in the rose-garden.

I have had my share of Dutch elm disease, and as I write, in the late autumn of 1972, I do not know whether that grim battle has been finally won, though the matter is in capable hands. Most of the tall old elms still stand, and it is hoped to save them in the spring by means of fungicidal injection. Meantime the tawny owls perch in their branches at dusk, and the grey squirrels scamper by day.

Except at weekends I am almost always alone, but that, also, is the way I like it. I discovered very early on, in my twenties, that the shared life was not for me, and that I should never have attempted it, since even as a young girl I declared that if ever I were to marry it would be to a sailor, as he would be most of the time away at sea, and when he came home I would be pleased to see him—for a little while, and then he would go away again for a long time. In this I have never changed. There are people who are naturally solitary—what Melville, in *Moby Dick,* called *isolatos*—those who 'did not acknowledge the common continent of men, but each *Isolato* living on a separate continent of his own'. From childhood to old age I have always been an *isolato.* I do not think it is either a good thing or a bad thing; it is a purely individual thing. Like a preference or a distaste for sugar in your tea. Or even an aversion to tea either way. I have, myself, a great aversion to family life. It is, in fact, one of my ideas of hell. But also I have a great respect for the Family, and a great admiration for those who have the gift to make a success of family life, people who marry and raise up a family and are happy in their marital partnership and the family life, and stay that way. It is a good 'design for living'—the most satisfactory there is, but it does call for particular qualifications of character and temperament which amount to a gift; a kind of grace.

I was never given the grace; I never wanted it. I wanted always to be free; the cat that walked alone. 'In the wild wet woods'; yes, I know, but the woods are not always wild and wet; and even when they are at least you can *breathe* in them ...

For some of us to be lived-with would be claustrophobic; suffocating.

Which does not mean that we do not like people and do not sometimes wish for company. An *isolato* is necessarily a misogamist, but a hatred of marriage is not a hatred of one's fellow man. Mostly I am very well content to be alone, and I am only innerly lonely, but there are days when on a great up-surge of longing I think, 'If only I could see my daughter!' But she has her life to live, in far-away Devon, with her little girl, and I have mine in London, and we meet when we can—which is not often, but we are all the time in touch, by letter and telephone.

In the Noël Coward revue running at the Mermaid Theatre as I write this there is a party scene in which someone declares, in the twenties manner, 'Life was made for living!', which produces the slightly bored reply that 'It's difficult to see, really, what else you *could* do with it!'

To which my own reaction is, Quite. For there comes a point when, with not so much of it left, it becomes important to do the best you can with it—though just how to is not always very clear. Perhaps it is nothing more complicated than getting along as best you can, and paying not too much attention to time passing. William Saroyan, whom by and large I admire—though he can talk an awful lot of nonsense—says in his *Days of Life and Death and Escape to the Moon*,* that if you think about time it's gone, but if you forget it it's always there. The thing is, as Saroyan says, 'I'm still alive, and everybody else keeps dying'.

Only it's not cause for congratulation as Saroyan seems to

* 1970.

o

think, but one of the bad and sad things about being old—the way people drop out all along the line. Even when you do not see old friends, and are perhaps never likely to see them again, it is nevertheless comforting that they are *there* and you are in touch with them. So far as I am concerned it is not important to see people; what is important is that they should be there, part of the background of one's life, as one is of theirs. It is pleasant to meet occasionally, but it is not essential. Only in the intimate, nearest-and-dearest circle is it essential, the lack of it a deprivation.

I have a friend, a Franciscan father, called in religion Father Angelo, whom I have not seen for twenty odd years, since we sheltered together from the rain under a fuchsia hedge in Connemara, and whom I am not likely to see again, for he is now in a friary in Scotland, but with whom, down through the years, I have kept in touch. The friendship is alive and well both sides of the Border. It would not gain anything if we met and chatted over cups of tea. It is very well the way it is. We remember each other's birthdays; we exchange letters in which I tell him of the books I am writing or have recently had published, and he in turn tells me of small excursions made with his elderly sister, or Father This or That. He has been, now, over sixty years in religion, and I have been nearly fifty years in authorship. We shall neither of us ever see again the running flame of a fuchsia hedge in Connemara, but it doesn't matter; we have seen, and blessed are our eyes.

Father Angelo is ahead of me along the road; if he drops out first I shall be sad, and lay an imaginary spray of wild fuschia on his memory; if I drop out first he will find comfort in praying for my soul, in accordance with his religious beliefs; I am sceptical of this doing me any good, but if, as I think, prayer does nothing for the prayed-for I am sure it does something for those who pray. Father Angelo belongs, really, to the first part of this book, the Irish section, but here he is, now, turning up at the end; but it makes sense, for all the Irish life was finished years ago, whereas the continuing friendship with my old friend of the fuchsia hedge in the rain is part of today's quiet rhythm.

3

At Close of Play

On and off there are travel fantasies: it is anyhow the cheapest form of travel, and makes none of the exhausting physical demands of the real thing. When in the summer of 1972 I read James Plunkett's lovely book about Ireland, *The Gems She Wore*, in which he quotes Yeats' letter to me concerning his epitaph, and after we had corresponded about Yeats and the book, I thought I would like to revisit Dublin and meet Plunkett, and that Joe O'Halloran would come up from Galway and we'd talk ourselves black in the face, as they say in the West, about books and people, with a great laugh—the way it hadn't been possible twelve years ago—about Mrs. Pandit's non-visit to the Literary Society; and I thought that as well as all this I would like to walk up O'Connell Street again—the 'street of the adulterers'—and across the bridge over the Liffey, and up Grafton Street, with its good shops, to St. Stephen's Green, with its statue of Constance Gore-Booth, 'Madame', the Countess Markiewicz, of heroic memory; and it would be fine to see Dublin Bay again, the long peninsula of Howth, and Killiney Bay, and the Dublin Mountains, and the view from the Hell Fire Club at the top. Nostalgia surged in me with the thought of it all; Dublin, like Paris, is a city to go back to; ever and always.

But I didn't go, though I took the trouble to find out about day-sailings to Dun Laoghaire, and the current cost of a room-with-bath in Dublin. I would go in the autumn, I thought, when I had finished *Stories from My Life*. But September and October came and went and in November I was still working on the book; then I told myself I had left it too late, and 'I'll go in the spring'. Well, I might; but there would have to be some sort of direct incentive, I think, as when I suddenly up-and-went to Paris to meet my old friend from California. Lacking any strong and direct incentive I will more likely just dream along; the charm of fantasy is that it demands no action. Action demands energy, and energy, when you become old, is in short supply. That there are people much older than oneself who fly off to the other side of the world as though it were no more than a trip to Brighton or Blackpool is neither here nor there. We are all different in this matter of energy—which is mental and nervous as well as physical.

I knew an Australian woman some years ago who travelled to England, by ship and alone, when she was eighty, for no other reason than that she had never been there before and thought it was about time. She stayed alone in a London hotel, went to Harrods and bought clothes, and when I escorted her here and there invariably told me how much better everything was in Sydney, which she called Seedney. 'Now in Seedney,' she was always saying. Still, although the London shops, traffic arrangements, public buildings, were not as good as in Seedney, she enjoyed herself, and planned, when she returned home, to look for a house by the sea—'for when I am reely old,' she said. She found it, too, lived in it, happily for about two years, then, in a moment of inattention, it seemed, she died.

At a luncheon party, too, not long ago, I met a remarkably well-preserved man of eighty and his sixtyish-seeming seventy-five-year-old wife who were still charging about in the Far East and had just returned from Pakistan and by no means considered they had been there for the last time.

I find it admirable, but also a little frightening, something in oneself protesting, 'The old monsters! Why can't they stay put?' No reason why they should, of course, since they have the energy to up-and-go. But, as with sex, there's this feeling that there's a time to call a halt—that, as the old limerick has it, 'there's a proper time for gaieties'. That sense, I suppose, of there being a time to rise up and go and a time to stay still; a time for living and a time for dying.

When the sun shines and I feel well there are upsurges of mental and physical energy in which I plan not only to revisit Dublin but to tramp round the ramparts of St. Malo again, see Venice once more, before the 'world's most beautiful drawing-room' sinks into the sea, and even indulge in fantasies of repeating the American journey in order to see the Grand Canyon from the other—and less frequented—side. There are places I have not seen and would have been interested to see —outstandingly the Great Wall of China. But it's too late now, and it doesn't matter; I have seen enough. I am glad to have seen the Taj Mahal, and had a glimpse of Everest, and walked round Rangoon's golden Shwe Dagon pagoda. I am glad to have seen the Grand Canyon, and the Petrified Forest, and San Francisco, and the wonderful redwood trees in Marin County across the Bay. I am glad to have been to Samarkand whilst it was still a forbidden and difficult journey, and to Jerusalem before it became Zionist-Occupied Territory. I am glad to have been in Mandalay, to have stayed in Japanese inns, and 'gone after tiger' on elephant-back in the Indian jungles. I am glad to have been a *traveller*, in the years before tourism, devoid of adventure. There was the authentic thrill in journeying when it was done the 'hard way', by boat and train, which was also the interesting way, the exciting and romantic way. Now there are merely 'flights', and monstrous airports, vast and impersonal, where human beings are herded like cattle and 'processed' like peas. I know a man whose idea of Heaven is Harrods through all eternity; I have no conception of Heaven—it is outside my reckoning—but my idea of Hell is Heathrow Airport. (I came to this conclusion long, long before I achieved the allotted span; I many years ago developed a horror of the place—almost a kind of *fear*—because of its vast, inexorable impersonality. I was last there in November, 1966, returning from Damascus, and by the grace of God and my own efforts I shall not make this Descent to Avernus again.)

I was interested in an article in *The Times* (November 9, 1972) by their environment correspondent, Tony Aldous, on what he called the 'Modern Cult of Earthshrinking', and in which he wrote of its cultural and social dangers. He disliked, as I also did, the BOAC's series of advertisements showing 'doll-like, plasticised British tourists', in shorts and pith helmets, 'about to be whisked to the four corners of the world, lured by package-tour or other cheap tariffs to spend 10 days or so sampling the exotic sights and sensations previously available only to the wealthy or determined.' He declares that one of the reasons for disliking these advertisements 'apart from their tastelessness', was the 'foreboding, born of experience, that the exotic does not often withstand exposure to the package-tour blight'. What this blight produces he defines as 'an edited version of local reality, which is in turn, by none too subtle commercial pressures distorting that reality into a universal "paella and chips" environment'. He cites a valuable book by Patrick Rivers, *The Restless Generation; a Crisis in Mobility,** and speaks of its 'frightening clarity'. Rivers declares that cheap mobility is the new cult, with the result that variety has become one of the first major casualties— 'Destinations draw closer as their worth diminishes'.

Tony Aldous speaks of a 'kind of cultural law of diminishing returns', so that 'by the time the ordinary tourist can afford to go to Corfu or Samarkand, budget hotels with Eurocardboard menus and Intourist or regulation Inthinglist guides have taken over'.

I am glad I got to Samarkand, in 1935, and dossed down on a bench on the railway station, having no place to go, since I was there illegally, from lack of a permit. It was a far from 'golden journey', but it was an adventure; it was *achievement*.

I have travelled a good deal in England during the last few years, making long journeys by train—more often than not there-and-back-in-a-day—to collect material for my three books about England, the first of which, *England for a Change*, published in 1968, derived its title from a question that was half suggestion, half protest, from my then editor at Hutchinson's, Cherry Kearton—'Why don't you write a book about *England*—for a *change*?' As a change, he meant, from books

* 1972.

about the Far East and the Middle East; I laughed, and exclaimed, 'What a good title that would make—*England for a Change*!' I said I would think about it—but between the stirrup and the English ground there was the impulse to go to California, and my next book was *An American Journey*, published in 1967. I did the American journey in the spring of 1966, and Damascus at the end of that year, but in 1967 I began rediscovering England, from Cornwall to Hadrian's Wall, from the Chesil Bank and Portland Bill to the Brontë country, with Hampshire and Edward Thomas country in between—not to mention Farnham and Cobbett country, and a voyage of discovery to Wigan-after-Orwell. I followed *England for a Change* with *England at Large* two years later, in 1970, and *England my Adventure* in 1972. I enjoyed rediscovering England, and it was exciting to find that so much of 'old England' remained, not yet despoiled by 'development' and motor-ways—though for how much longer I wonder, for even when old towns and villages have escaped the horrors of these forms of pollution the narrow streets are everywhere choked with traffic, and the foundations of old buildings racked by the weight of it. Not to mention the threat to ancient cathedrals from the vibrations of the overflying—and increasingly huge and numerous—'planes. Perhaps there is a last-look-at-England still to be recorded before Foulness becomes an airport, and many a lovely village is riven by the M-this, the A-that, and many a field and orchard swallowed up in urban spread. I make no plans; when you are a writer all waits upon inspiration—using that word not in any highfalutin' sense but in the sense of incentive, the impulse of an idea, the sparking of imagination.

I have been a socialist all my adult life, from the age of fifteen, and now, at close of play, in the seventies, am more than ever convinced of the necessity for social revolution. Since the mid-thirties, and the Spanish Civil War, I have taken my stand with the anarchists, opposed to all forms of *centralised* government, and profoundly mistrusting all political parties. Communism, as practised by the U.S.S.R., is obviously what young Cohen Bendit calls 'obsolete'. Cohen Bendit's book, *Obsolete*

Communism, the Left-Wing Alternative, published in 1968, after the May Revolution in Paris that year, the 'Second Revolution', stands on my political shelf next to Che Guevara's *Bolivian Diary,* published after his death. In the concluding chapter of his book, with its sub-title, *C'est pour toi que tu fais la revolution,* Cohen Bendit declares, 'There is only one reason for being a revolutionary—because it is the best way to live.' He speaks of the 'premature' revolution of 1968, and the 'crisis of our culture', attributable to the capitalist system of society and its basic contradictions, and concludes that 'the last word has not yet been said'. Well, it certainly has not; what we are witnessing now is the crisis of capitalism itself; it is self-evidently no longer a viable economic—let alone social—system. We are witnessing its protracted death, but my generation, I suspect, will not live to see it dead and buried; the capitalist confederation of the Common Market will sustain it a while longer yet. But only for a while.

I am glad to have lived to see the end of the British Empire, and a number of countries liberate themselves from imperialism and achieve independence—that some of them have made a mess of that independence is a very great pity, but it is their own affair. If I can hold on for a few more years I might live to see a united Ireland—a thirty-two-county Irish Republic. I worked in the anti-partition movement with the London Irish before the war, but after the war it seemed a lost cause, until recently, when the issue, like the Palestine issue since 1967, is out in the open and can be discussed and debated, where once only a handful of people knew or cared. Now it is at least possible to hope. The hope for Palestine is more remote, and I think it unlikely that I shall live to see this cause, the one I have most intensely at heart, triumphant, with Palestine as *Palestine* again, with the indigenous people, the Palestinian Arabs, in control, a nation again, Moslem and Christian, co-existing with a Jewish minority. It will come, but not, I think, for another twenty years or so yet—and I cannot wait so long.

More important than putting men on the moon is the establishment of justice and reason here on earth; but, fantastically, it is easier to put men on the moon—which benefits no one.

When I switched on my little transistor set—all the radio I have—the other night, ahead of the news, which is about all I listen to, I heard a voice saying, fretfully, 'I want my life to mean *something*!' I was interested in the stress; to me it would have made more sense if it had been on 'mean'—to *mean* something. Though I am of those who think that life has no meaning; there is something called life and we are part of it and have to cope with it as best we can. Sometimes it seems good to us, and sometimes dreary, and sometimes sheer hell. There's no equality and no justice; never has been; but one day, perhaps . . .

There have been a great many stories in my life, of places and people and experiences, and most of them have gone into books, or been used as material for stories; this book concludes all the hitherto unrecorded stories from my life I want to commit to paper autobiographically, but life itself is a continuing story, and, as they say up North, you never know what's round t'next bloody corner . . . which is just as well.

Epilogue, 1973

It was at a local 'bus stop. There were only the two of us, an elderly man and myself. It was a grey day with a cold wind and we waited and we waited, the unending stream of cars and vans and lorries continually bearing down on us and hurtling past, but never a 'bus in sight, and finally I spoke my thought aloud—'The joys of public transport!' I said, bitterly.

The man was more philosophic.

'All held up in the Putney High Street bottleneck, I suppose,' he said, then added, boldly, 'I've often seen you about!'

'I've been about in this area for the last forty-five years,' I told him. 'You can say I'm one of the local sights!'

Then we both exclaimed, 'Ah! At last!'

We held up our hands as the 'bus lumbered alongside and when we boarded sat together because it worked out like that. When we were settled, our fares collected, the man said, 'You know, for years I thought you were Ethel Mannin!'

Had I been smart I should have said, 'Good God, no! Surely not that one!' That might really have been interesting; instead, I said, helplessly, 'I'm sorry to disappoint you, but I am!'

He stared at me.

'*No!*' he said. '*Really?* I mean—that lovely black hair parted in the middle—I'll always remember all those photographs in the papers!'

'I always came out dark in the photographs,' I said, sombrely. 'In fact I had golden hair. Now, as you can see, I'm a faded blonde.' I added, for full measure, 'We don't go grey

in our family. My father didn't. He had that golden fair hair.
We just dingily fade.'

But he wasn't listening; only staring.

'So you really are—Ethel Mannin?'

'Afraid so,' I said, somewhere between wry amusement and
resentment at the incredulity. Hell, did one have to produce
some kind of identification card to convince a stranger?

'Still writing?' he inquired.

Never a good question to put to a writer.

'Book out a few weeks ago,' I said curtly. 'The High Street
bookshop has it.' I told him the title.

'Well!' he said.

A number of people got on at the next stop, and it was
standing-room-only, and a good deal of push and shove, not
conducive to conversation, but he volunteered, as the various
bodies arranged themselves and we jerked and jolted on again,
'I'm an artist.'

Not knowing the answer to that I smiled. Thinly. Mercifully at the next stop he struggled to his feet.

He said, 'It's been very nice meeting you.'

I smiled. Bleakly.

It ought to be end-of-story; at the time I thought it was. I told
it to a number of people and they all thought it Terribly
Funny.

But as it turned out it was not end-of-story, for some weeks
later I recounted it to the manageress of an off-licence I
patronise, she being a fan of mine, and never for a moment
doubting from the word go that I was the author of all those
lovely books. Also, bless her, loyally denying, in the face of the
living evidence, that I had Changed All That Much in the last
fifty years.

I told her the story of the man who had for years always
thought I was Ethel Mannin, and whilst she was still rolling
about behind the counter with laughter a woman standing
next to me, clutching her bottle and waiting her turn to be
rung up on the till, also laughed and chipped in with, 'I can
understand it—I mean the hairstyle's the same . . .'

End of story. Absolutely.

Index

Abdullah, King of Jordan, 80
Adams, Michael, 47
Aldous, Tony, 213–14
Alexandria, 99, 101, 119–20
Al Fatah, 86
Amin, Adel (Egyptian lawyer),
  62 et seq., 119–20
Arab Bureau for Cinema, 64 et
  seq.
Arab League, 70 et seq.
Arif, Colonel Abdul Salam, 179,
  181, 185, 189, 191, 203
Aswan, 201
Athens, 109 et seq.
Austin, Rickey, 123 et seq., 169,
  191, 212

Ba'ath party, 86, 179
Babylon, 111
Bach, Johann Sebastian, 160 et
  seq.
Baghdad, 15, 55, 56, 66, 180 et
  seq.
Bairam, Muslim festival, 119
Barada, river, 86 et seq.
Barbour, Nevill, 74
Basrah, 45, 47, 192
Bedouins, of Jordan, 77 et seq.
Beersheba, 81, 84
Beethoven, Ludwig von, 160
Benares, 114
Bennett, Arnold, 112, 113

Bertrand Russell Foundation, 181,
  182, 185, 186, 192
Bhalla, Rattan, 26, 29
Boyd-Orr, John, 1st Baron,
  183
Brockway, Fenner, Lord, 183
Brogan, Patrick, 133
Burma, 31 et seq. (see also
  Rangoon, Mandalay)
Bustani, Emile, 49, 58
Byron, George Gordon, 6th
  Baron, 113

Cairo, 82 et seq., 108, 188
California, 191, 202 (see also Los
  Angeles, San Francisco)
Calman, Mel, 205
Capitalism, crisis of, 216
Carcassonne, 118
Castro, Fidel, 193
Chesterton, G. K., 160
Chorley, Lord, 1st Baron of
  Kendal, 183
Christie, Agatha, 206
Cohen Bendit, Daniel, 215–16
Connemara, 13 et seq., 205,
  210
Conrad, Joseph, 206
Corfu, 214
Corinth, canal, 109
Cotton, H. E. M., Colonel, 30
Coward, Sir Noël, 209

Damascus, 86 et seq.
Dhahiriya, Jordan, 81, 84
Debussy, Claude, 160
Dickinson, Emily, 206
Dublin, 211
Durrell, Lawrence, 108

Elgin, Thomas Bruce, 7th earl, 112
Eliot, T. S., 170
England, rediscovery of, 215

Failaka, island, 59 et seq.
Faulks, Jean (author's daughter),
    155, 190, 209
Fermor, Patrick, 108

Galway, 14, 23 et seq.
Gaza Strip, 46, 56–7
Glubb, Sir John Bagot, 90
Goethe, Johan Wolfgang von,
    199, 200
Gogarty, Oliver St. John, 25
Gollancz, Sir Victor, 107
Gore-Booth, Constance (Madame
    Markiewicz), 211
Grand Canyon, 213
Greene, Graham, 205
Griffiths, Will, M.P., 182 et seq.,
    188
Guevara, Ernesto 'Che', 190,
    192, 193, 261

Hale, Leslie, M.P., 183–4
Hatem, Dr. A. K., 63 et seq.
Haworth, 146–7
Heathrow Airport, 213
Hebron, 77 et seq., 84, 90 et seq.
Higham, Sir Charles, 37
Hurst, Desmond Brian, 69 et seq.
Hussein, King of Jordan, 65, 68,
    70, 71, 75–6, 84
Husseini, Musa, 79

Ibrahim, Fathi, 63 et seq.
Iraq, 15, 45, 58, 111, 148, 150,
    180, 189 (see also Baghdad,
    Basrah)

Iraqi Students' Society, 179 et
    seq., 193
Ireland, Republic of, 13 et seq.,
    216 (see also Dublin, Galway,
    Connemara, Kildare)
'Israel', 86
Israelis, 84–5, 93 et seq.

Japan, 36, 113, 207
Jericho, 74, 75, 94
Jerusalem, 74, 78, 83, 84–5, 91,
    94, 114, 213
Jordan, 74 et seq., 84 (see also
    Jerusalem, Hebron, Bethlehem,
    Jericho)

Kearton, Cherry, 214–15
Kildare, 35 et seq.
Kurds, the, 185, 191
Kuwait, State of, 45 et seq., 65,
    73

Leeds, 146–7, 148
Los Angeles, 202
Lydda, 75, 90, 92

McNulty, Rev. Hugh (Fr.
    Angelo, O.F.M.), 210
Makarios, President, 115
Mandalay, 213
Mannin, Edith (author's mother),
    204
Mannin, Robert (author's father),
    197, 204, 220
Maugham, W. Somerset, 198–9,
    201, 206
Melville, Herman, 208
Messmer, Pierre, 133
Michelangelo, 200
Montagu, Dr. Ashley, 67
Morocco, 83
Mozart, Wolfgang Amadeus, 160
Muggeridge, Malcolm, 100

Nasser, Gamal Abdul, 67, 76, 185
Nehru, Jawaharlal, 25, 30
New York, 202

Nubian desert, 201–2
Nuri es-Said, 183

O'Donovan, Capt. Donal, 29
O'Halloran, P. J., 25 et seq., 211
Ortega y Gasset, Jose, 199

Palestine Conference, 216
Palestine Liberation Organisation, 74, 83
Palestinians, in Kuwait, 48
Pandit, Mrs. Lakshmi Vijaya, 25 et seq., 211
Paris, 123 et seq., 188, 211–12
Petrified Forest, the, 213
Piraeus, 108, 109, 113
Plunkett, James, 211
Pompidou, President, 128, 133
Prendergast, Mrs. Tona, 27, 29

Qassim, Abdel Karim, General, 15, 45, 47, 55–6, 58, 65, 148, 150, 179 et seq.

Rabat, 83
Ramallah, 90, 91
Rangoon, 173, 213
Ravel, Maurice, 160
Reed, Henry, 203
Rees, Tudor, 138
Revolution, necessity of, 215
Reynolds, Reginald, 14, 25, 51, 74, 79, 137 et seq., 204
Rivers, Patrick, 214
Royden, Maude, 149
Rhodes, 115, 117 et seq.
Russell, Bertrand, 3rd Earl, 185

Sabah, Sheikh Abdullah Al-Salam Al Sabah, 46, 55 et seq.
Sabah tribe, 46
St. Malo, Britanny, 213
Samarkand, 213, 214
San Francisco, 213

Saroyan, William, 209–10
Schoenman, Ralph, 192
Sevrez, Helen, 37
Shammout, Ismael, 83
Sheridan, Clare, 24, 25
Shiber, Dr. George, 51–2, 60
Shivaramakrishnan, M. R., 27 et seq.
Siam, Ali, 65 et seq.
Society of Friends (Quakers), 138
Spanish Civil War, 215
Squire, Sir John, 140

Taj Mahal, 213
Tannous, Dr. Izzat, 51
Tourism, pollution of, 213–14
Tropic of Cancer, 201
Turner, Gilbert, 151, 156

United Nations, 185
United Nations Works and Relief Agency (U.N.W.R.A.), 56, 57, 82
U.S.S.R., 215

Venice, 99, 101 et seq., 213

Wadi Halfa, 201
Wagner, Richard, 160
White, T. H., 107, 108
Wigan, 152
Windsor, 156 et seq.
World War I, 47, 46, 47
World War II, 32, 33, 46

Yeats, W. B., 24, 25, 211
Yugoslavia, 101

Zaki, Khalid, 179 et seq.
Zen Buddhism, 39, 40
Ziemsen, F. W. ('Tim'), 156 et seq., 161 et seq., 208
Zionism, 63, 156 et seq., 168 et seq., 208